GREAT POOLS, SPAS
& OUTDOOR LIVING

MEREDITH₊ BOOKS
DES MOINES, IOWA

Great Pools, Spas & Outdoor Living
Editor: Vicki Christian
Contributing Writers: Amber Barz, Jan Walker
Contributing Graphic Designer: Sundie Ruppert, Studio G
Assistant Art Director: Erin Burns
Copy Chief: Terri Fredrickson
Publishing Operations Manager: Karen Schirm
Senior Editor, Asset & Information Management: Phillip Morgan
Edit and Design Production Coordinator: Mary Lee Gavin
Editorial Assistant: Kaye Chabot
Book Production Managers: Pam Kvitne, Marjorie J. Schenkelberg,
    Rick von Holdt, Mark Weaver
Contributing Copy Editor: Jane Woychick
Contributing Proofreaders: Juliet Jacobs, David Krause, Candy Meier
Cover Photographer: Joan Hix Vanderschult
Contributing Indexer: Stephanie Reymann

Meredith® Books
Executive Director, Editorial: Gregory H. Kayko
Executive Director, Design: Matt Strelecki
Managing Editor: Amy Tincher-Durik
Executive Editor: Benjamin W. Allen
Senior Editor/Group Manager: Vicki Leigh Ingham
Senior Associate Design Director: Mick Schnepf
Marketing Product Manager: Brent Wiersma

Publisher and Editor in Chief: James D. Blume
Editorial Director: Linda Raglan Cunningham
Executive Director, New Business Development: Todd M. Davis
Executive Director, Sales: Ken Zagor
Director, Operations: George A. Susral
Director, Production: Douglas M. Johnston
Director, Marketing: Amy Nichols
Business Director: Jim Leonard

Vice President and General Manager: Douglas J. Guendel

Meredith Publishing Group
President: Jack Griffin
Senior Vice President: Karla Jeffries

Meredith Corporation
Chairman of the Board: William T. Kerr
President and Chief Executive Officer: Stephen M. Lacy

In Memoriam: E.T. Meredith III (1933–2003)

All of us at Meredith® Books are dedicated to providing you with information and ideas to enhance your home. We welcome your comments and suggestions. Write to us at: Meredith Books, Home Decorating and Design Editorial Department, 1716 Locust St., Des Moines, IA 50309-3023.

TABLE OF CONTENTS

INTRODUCTION

Ultimate outdoor living spaces go beyond a basic deck or patio to comfortably accommodate every aspect of daily life, from exercising, cooking, and entertaining to simply relaxing. These inviting retreats feature thoughtful layouts, lush landscaping, and the latest innovations in backyard pools and spas. Whether you want to share an intimate alfresco meal with family, throw lavish dinner parties under the stars, swim laps and splash in the pool with the kids, or just relax in a hot tub, you'll find a multitude of picture-perfect locations here.

For your reading ease, this book is divided into seven chapters that focus on a variety of outdoor accommodations.

CHAPTER ONE
PARTY BY THE POOL highlights poolside amenities and attractive surrounds perfect for exercising, entertaining, and rejuvenating spirits.

CHAPTER TWO
RELAX IN AN AHHH SPA, with backyard amenities such as hot tubs, lap pools, and more to pamper and indulge yourself and guests.

CHAPTER THREE
BRING THE INSIDE OUT shows how to bring a backyard landscape to life with the same style and class as featured in beautiful home interiors.

CHAPTER FOUR
FIND SERENITY WITH WATER spotlights exquisite locations adorned with bubbling fountains and other water features that create dreamlike ambiences.

CHAPTER FIVE
COZY UP TO THE FIRE showcases outdoor fireplaces and fire pits.

CHAPTER SIX
CREATE A COOK'S FANTASY includes alfresco kitchens that are as accommodating as their indoor counterparts, including the latest in grills, outdoor work surfaces, and more.

CHAPTER SEVEN
ENTERTAIN WITH FLAIR shows how to arrange a yard into enticing gathering spaces that make a couple or a crowd feel welcome and comfortable.

So get started. Turn the page to begin an armchair tour of some of the most incredible backyards you've ever seen. Then turn your dream into reality by transforming your backyard into your own personal haven.

8

chapter 1
Party
by the Pool

Moroccan Mood

With Mediterranean flair and sparkling water, a suburban patio Is Reborn as an exotic getaway.

LEFT PLANTS GROUPED TOGETHER ON A WIRE PLANT STAND ADD A PERSONAL TOUCH, AS WELL AS COLOR AND LIFE TO THE YARD.

OPPOSITE A SPA WITH A TINKLING FOUNTAIN SOOTHES THE SOUL AND OFFERS THE PERFECT LUXURIOUS RETREAT WHERE YOU CAN RELAX AND ENJOY THE GREAT OUTDOORS.

OPPOSITE A SMALL
SITTING AREA AT THE
POOL'S EDGE PROVIDES
A WONDERFUL PLACE TO
ENJOY THE LANDSCAPE.
.THE JETS, STAINED-
CONCRETE PATIO, AND
SCULPTED ARCHES
CREATE AN EXOTIC LOOK.

ABOVE LEFT A
MOSQUITO-NETTING
CANOPY SURROUNDS
AN ITALIAN CHAISE TO
ENHANCE THE EXOTIC
LOOK OF THE LANDSCAPE.

ABOVE RIGHT A
STAINLESS-STEEL GRILL
AND SMALL OUTDOOR BAR
CREATE AN INVITING NOOK
FOR ENJOYING DELICIOUS
BARBECUE WITH FRIENDS
AND FAMILY.

Sit poolside at a tile-top cafe table overlooking graceful Moroccan arches and allow the soothing sounds of fountains to wash away the stress of the day. You can do it from your own patio if you take your cue from the Mediterranean getaway that sits in a Dallas suburb.

The exotic space, housed inside a narrow suburban backyard, is as alluring as any indoor space. Sculpted yellow arches frame a colorful mosaic-tile mural. The sturdy walls offer privacy and a sense of the Mediterranean as they stretch around the perimeter.

Streaming water flowing from below the arches lends a waterfall-like appearance, but can also be turned off for a quieter environment. Running water is a continuous theme as jets spray water into the pool and a fountain bubbles in the spa's center.

The stained concrete patio resembles ancient stone floors. Mosquito-netting canopies and Italian chaises offer a tropical place to relax. Wrought-iron dining chairs mesh perfectly with the Moroccan style of the yard and offer a nice place to enjoy an afternoon snack or bask in the warm sun. A stainless-steel grill atop the bar provides an excellent place to cook up a delicious evening meal and looks right at home in the yard.

Potted green plants and colorful flowers dotted throughout the landscape bring this area all together and give the mostly hard-surface yard a touch of life.

Water's Edge

A MAGNIFICENT HILLTOP VIEW INSPIRES A DREAMLIKE POOL WITH AN EDGE THAT VANISHES INTO THIN AIR.

LEFT A ROCK PLACED AT THE POOL'S EDGE APPEARS TO BE A NATURAL PART OF THE LANDSCAPE BUT ACTUALLY DISGUISES PLUMBING.

OPPOSITE A SPA TUCKED NEXT TO THE VANISHING-EDGE POOL PROVIDES AN IDEAL SPOT TO WATCH THE SUNSET AND ENJOY THE VIEW.

This hilltop pool provides an escape from the everyday and a place to enjoy a magnificent view. The vanishing edge of this pool makes it appear as though the water drops off into a canyon. (For more information on vanishing-edge pools, see pages 38–41.) Black onyx pebbles on the bottom of the pool make the pool look deeper and more like a lake than a pool. Stones and boulders along the edges add to the natural look of the pool and enhance the surroundings.

Tiles in earthy tones border the pool, distinguishing it from the patio yet keeping the nature theme alive. Blooming flowers and tall trees soften the hard lines of the pool and patio.

Plush, comfortable lounge chairs situated on the patio offer loungers a perfect place to take in the sunset or enjoy a quiet afternoon by the water. A kitchen area equipped with a stove, grill, bar, and sink invite family and friends to enjoy a mouthwatering meal with a magnificent backdrop. Gurgling fountains at opposite ends of the pool add serenity to the landscape.

OPPOSITE A VANISHING-EDGE POOL CREATES THE ILLUSION THAT THE POOL WATER FLOWS OVER THE FAR EDGE AND DROPS TO THE CANYON BELOW.

ABOVE AN OUTDOOR KITCHEN GIVES EVERYONE A TABLE WITH A SPECTACULAR VIEW.

Exotic Escape

BREAK FROM THE ORDINARY AND ENJOY A WONDERLAND OF TROPICAL BEAUTY AS YOU ENTER THE BACKYARD.

LEFT THE BOSTON FERNS, VIBRANT CROTONS, AND BANANA TREES ADD A TOUCH OF LIFE TO THE AREA. THE DIFFERENT TEXTURES COMPLEMENT ONE ANOTHER AND THE SURROUNDINGS.

OPPOSITE WATER FLOWS GENTLY OVER THE EDGE OF THE SPA INTO THE POOL. THE CABANA SITS NEXT TO THE POOL AND THE SPA FOR EASY ACCESS.

Tropical plants, a serene waterfall, and a Caribbean-blue pool turn a plain patio into a tranquil escape. The lush plants with their different textures and sizes that appeal to the eye entice visitors to the backyard. A sand-color concrete patio underfoot offers contrast to the greenery and provides ample space for seating.

Lounge chairs at the poolside provide a quaint place for relaxing in the afternoon sun. Easily transportable umbrellas placed along the patio make lounging or dining something that can be done in the warmth of the sun or the cool of the shade. The lounge chairs, dining seats, and umbrella visually tie together the seating area.

A waterfall spilling gently from the spa into the pool adds the soothing sounds of running water and complements the naturalistic feel of the yard. The bubbling spa is separated from the pool by the waterfall, with flat stones setting the backdrop. The cabana fits perfectly into the corner of the landscape and is close to both pool and spa to ensure easy access. The oversize roof provides extra shade during the day and lighting that can be switched on after the sun has gone down. The yard creates an instant vacation for everyone who enters the space.

OPPOSITE Chaise LOUNGE CHAIRS PROVIDE A COMFY SPOT NEXT TO THE POOL TO TAKE IN THE WATER, BLOOMING PLANTS, AND PRACTICAL CABANA.

ABOVE NATURAL STONE AND LUSH GREENERY SURROUNDING THE SPA CREATE A NATURAL AND OUTDOORSY LOOK.

Carefree Spirit

Your tropical island fantasies can come true with these azure waters and lush plantings.

LEFT A SMALL WATERFALL BUILT INTO A PLANTER CREATES CALMING SOUNDS SURE TO TAKE AWAY WORKDAY STRESSES.

OPPOSITE A LARGE HAMMOCK HUNG BESIDE THE POOL OFFERS AN ENTICING TROPICAL GETAWAY IN A PRIVATE SUBURBAN BACKYARD.

OPPOSITE PALM TREES DECORATING THE EDGES OF THE LANDSCAPE PROVIDE SHADE AS WELL AS PRIVACY.

TOP LEFT A GRILL BUILT INTO A BAR NEAR THE POOL MAKES OUTDOOR COOKING CONVENIENT AND ALLOWS THE COOK TO BE A PART OF THE PARTY.

TOP RIGHT NATURAL STONES SURROUND THE SPA, ALLOWING WATER TO CASCADE SMOOTHLY OVER THE STONES INTO THE POOL.

Lush tropical plants and a hammock give this backyard an exotic beach ambience. The cool blue of the pool is enticing in the hot summer sun and beckons people of all ages to jump in and cool down. Water flowing from the spa into the pool as well as through a small waterfall, creates a serene trickling sound that echoes through the yard.

An overhead trellis and tall palm trees ensure shade from the sun and enhance the beautiful tropical scene. A hammock strung between two of the trees offers a perfect place to lounge after a dip in the pool, and gives an exotic feel to the landscape.

A cozy seating area shaded by a large umbrella provides an ideal place to enjoy an evening meal cooked up on the large grill in the outdoor kitchen.

After dinner the warm spa beckons guests to enjoy a glass of wine and unwind after a long day. Tropical plants and cheerful blooms strewn throughout the landscape add color and life.

Containers filled with colorful blooms are easy to move and allow you to rearrange flowers for a sense of change. The colorful plants and refreshing water ensure that everyone can enjoy the yard on a warm day.

Desert Oasis

A PRIVATE PARADISE FEATURES A PEBBLED SURFACE POOL, GRACEFUL WATERFALLS, AND ABUNDANT GREENERY.

LEFT CONNECTICUT BLUESTONE COPING SURROUNDS THE EDGE OF THE POOL, CREATING A SMOOTH TRANSITION FROM PEBBLES TO PATIO.

OPPOSITE THE ROLLING HILLS OF THIS CALIFORNIA LANDSCAPE CREATE THE PERFECT BACKDROP FOR A POND-SHAPE POOL WITH A FAUX-BEACH ENTRY.

LEFT THE SPA IS SET SLIGHTLY ABOVE THE POOL, SURROUNDED BY ROCKS AND BOULDERS TO SET IT APART. A GENTLE WATERFALL MAKES BOTH WATER FEATURES LOOK NATURAL.

RIGHT SPECTACULAR GREENERY SURROUNDS THE POOL. BOULDERS DOT THE EDGE, ADDING CHARACTER AND SERVING AS PRIME LAUNCHING SPOTS FOR DIVERS.

Finished entirely with a surface of small pebbles, this inground saltwater pool in California invites visitors and the family dog to wade right in. Soft curves around a nontraditionally shaped pool help make the landscape appear more natural.

Greenery surrounding the pool and flanking the sides of an outdoor waterfall and spa provides a little privacy as well as eye-catching blooms. Water gently flowing down the waterfall and from the spa to the pool adds a serene sound to the area. Boulders placed strategically around the pool keep in tune with nature and offer a fun place to launch into the pool from above. The boulders continue as a backdrop for the waterfall and spa and tie the landscape together. (CONTINUED ON PAGE 30)

Patio and pool are tied together by using the same Connecticut bluestone that provides the perfect transition from pebbled pool to smooth patio. Seating beneath a grass-top hut ensures an escape to the shade, and the hut entices visitors with its fun structure. Additional lounge chairs around the patio provide comfortable areas for relaxing and catching some rays. Another patio next to the house offers seating for an evening meal as well as a beautiful view of the landscape.

ABOVE SMALL PEBBLES ON THE BOTTOM SURFACE GIVE THIS SALTWATER POOL THE FEEL OF A MINIATURE BEACH.

OPPOSITE A GRASS-TOP HUT BRINGS THE ALLURE OF THE BEACH TO THE PATIO AND OFFERS SHADE FOR SWIMMERS TOWELING OFF FROM THE POOL.

Casual Cabana

THIS ENTICING RETREAT UNIFIES HOUSE AND YARD WITH SIMPLE AND LOVELY DESIGN ELEMENTS.

LEFT ITALIAN GLASS MOSAIC TILES ON THE INSIDE OF THE POOL GIVES THE WATER A SPARKLING ALLURE.

OPPOSITE ROOF BEAMS OF DOUGLAS FIR STRETCH OUT BEYOND THE CABANA, CREATING A SHADED LOUNGE AREA PERFECT FOR DRYING OFF OR ENJOYING AN AFTERNOON OUTDOORS.

OPPOSITE TRICKLING WATER SPILLS OUT FROM THE SPA INTO THE POOL, INSTILLING A SENSE OF SERENITY THAT FLOWS THROUGHOUT THE LANDSCAPE.

ABOVE PLANTER BOXES NEAR THE POOL ARE SURROUNDED WITH THE SAME ROUNDED-EDGE CEMENT-PLASTER MATERIAL THAT WAS USED FOR THE PERIMETER WALLS.

ABOVE RIGHT SMOOTH GLASS MOSAIC TILES FORM A BACKREST ON THE TWO OUTER SIDES OF THE SPA. WARM WATER CASCADES OVER THE EDGE, SOOTHING THOSE SITTING BELOW.

Well-designed pools such as this one enhance their setting by following a unified theme. The pool and cabana were added to the backyard six years after the construction of the house. To marry the new outdoor space with the existing house, the new structures feature similar architectural lines and materials.

Rounded-edge walls are a design element used in the main house. Extending the look to the landscape provides visual continuity and privacy from near neighbors. The rounded edges surround the spa, pool, and planter boxes and extend from the cabana, fully unifying the area.

The extended roof beams of the cabana mimic the size and shape of beams used in the home's interior and offer selective shading. The spacious terra-cotta tile patio matches the flooring in a few interior spaces and provides an ideal place to enjoy an evening meal with family and friends after a fun afternoon outdoors.

Italian glass mosaic tiles on the bottom and sides of this pool are a departure from the main home; they were added to make the water a sparkling attraction sure to entice anyone on a warm afternoon. The tile stretches over the spa as well, making the two elements appear as one. Overflow from the spa into the pool creates a pocket of warm water for swimmers relaxing on the smooth tile bench that wraps around the spa.

Portable white umbrellas offer the option of shade or sun anywhere in the yard. Flower boxes filled with blooming plants add decorative touches to the landscape.

SOFT, ROUNDED-EDGE WALLS SURROUND THE POOL, ENSURING PRIVACY. THE PERIMETER WALLS MATCH THE EXTERIOR WALLS OF THE HOME. A TERRA-COTTA TILE PATIO HOSTS LOUNGE CHAIRS AND A POOLSIDE DINING TABLE READY FOR FAMILY OR GUESTS.

Personal Paradise

A VANISHING-EDGE POOL, NATURAL STONE PATIO, AND BUBBLING BROOK TRANSFORM A BASIC BACKYARD INTO A PRIVATE SANCTUARY.

LEFT A FIELDSTONE RETAINING WALL GIVES A BIT OF PRIVACY AND IS STILL IN KEEPING WITH THE NATURAL LOOK OF THE YARD.

OPPOSITE BOULDERS AT THE POOL'S EDGE MARK THE END OF THE POOL AND ALSO SERVE AS STEPPING STONES TO A SMALL ISLAND IN THE CENTER OF THE WATER.

PERSONAL PARADISE

A STONE PATIO POOL
SURROUND ENSURES
A NATURAL LOOK FOR
THE LANDSCAPE AND
CREATES PLENTY OF
SPACE FOR COMFORTABLE
LOUNGE CHAIRS. LARGE
UMBRELLAS OFFER
RELIEF FROM THE SUN.

Whether you call it a negative, infinity, illusion, or vanishing edge, there's no denying the appeal of a pool that drops away along one side to reveal a breathtaking view. A 45-foot long spillway that forms the back wall of this pool was specially designed to drop a few feet to incorporate the sound of running water.

The pool edge drops away to showcase a spectacular vista of rolling hills and natural water. A stone patio dotted with boulders surrounds the pool and gives the yard a natural feel. Lounge chairs across the patio offer comfortable spots to enjoy the view or relax in the sun or shade.

Lush greenery planted along the edge of the pool brings color to the area. A seating area along the backside of the pool is perfect for an afternoon snack and offers extra seating for any visitors. A retaining wall made of old fieldstones surrounds the entire escape and offers some privacy.

Playful Approach

SPICE UP YOUR BACKYARD WITH AN ORNATE POOL HOUSE, BUBBLING SPA, AND CURVACIOUS POOL.

LEFT A SPARKLING PLASTERLIKE COATING ON THE BOTTOM OF THE POOL GIVES THE FINISH AN APPEARANCE SIMILAR TO GRANITE. TILES OUTLINED WITH STONES CREATE THE PERFECT ACCENT ON THE STAIRS AND ADD A PERSONAL TOUCH.

OPPOSITE GREEN FOLIAGE AND A SUNSHINE YELLOW POOL HOUSE MAKE AN EYECATCHING COLOR COMBINATION.

GLASS BLOCKS CONNECT
POOL AND SPA AND
INTEGRATE THE TWO
WATER AREAS. PALM
TREES AND A WOODEN
FENCE SEPARATE THE
BACKYARD FROM A
NEIGHBORING PROPERTY.

In this South Carolina backyard, transplanted palm trees bring a tropical feel to the landscape and make the area feel like a vacation paradise. Tropical plants and blooming flowers sprinkled around the landscape liven up the scenery.

A yellow pool house offers a place to put on a swimsuit, shower, and get ready for some fun in the sun. Sound system controls are also located inside the building and connect via underground wire to weather-resistant speakers that look like rocks in the landscape. A large canopy extending over the pool house provides shade for the cozy seating area as well as the spa.

The sparkling blue pool bottom reflects the sun and makes the light dance off the water. Two sets of controls—one in the pool house and one in the main house—allow the owners to change the color of the pool lighting and control the flow of water.

River rock tiles cut into diamond shapes and outlined with jewel-color stones enliven the pool steps. Glass blocks along the edge of the spa add more sparkle, and a slightly lower ledge allows water to cascade over the edge into the pool.

Woodland Haven

A PRIVATE PARADISE COMES ALIVE WITH TOWERING TREES THAT ENSURE PRIVACY AND SHADE.

LEFT A PLANTING BED NEAR THE EDGE OF THE POOL OFFERS ANOTHER VISUAL CONNECTION TO NATURE'S BEAUTY.

OPPOSITE THE CURVED EDGE OF THE CUSTOM POOL RESEMBLES THE SHAPE OF A NATURAL LAGOON, CREATING HARMONY BETWEEN THE NATURAL AND ARTIFICIAL ELEMENTS OF THIS LANDSCAPE.

WOODLAND HAVEN

THE GAZEBO BY THE
POOL PROVIDES A NICE
PLACE TO ENJOY AN
OUTDOOR MEAL OR JUST
RELAX IN THE SHADE.
THE LUSH LANDSCAPE OF
MATURE TREES MAKES
THE BACKYARD FEEL
TRANQUIL AND PRIVATE.

If you are fortunate to live in a woodland setting, the surrounding landscape may provide the perfect backdrop for an enticing pool and gazebo.

Unite a pool with a woodland setting by using natural materials and soft landscaping. This Atlanta pool gets its fresh-from-nature feel from the decking crafted from flagstones and the sweeping planting pockets that surround the pool and patio.

For more visual integration, the white gazebo with a lake blue roof boasts the same colors as the house. A garden "island" appears to float in the pool and adds to the enticing beauty of the landscape. Offsetting the island, the gazebo also appears to float in the water. The entire landscape is tied together with wide flagstone walkways that create a link to every structure.

Traditional Treasure

Entertain guests all day and into the night in a classic backyard with comforting waters and an inviting pavilion.

LEFT This Asian fountain in the courtyard generates peaceful sounds perfectly suited to quiet meditation.

OPPOSITE The large pavilion can be arranged to accommodate intimate conversation as well as large parties.

A maze of brick courtyards and a covered pavilion make this Florida backyard feel like a vacation place in Europe. Elaborate architectural details such as hand-carved arched doors and vine-clad pillars add to the elegance of the yard.

Adorned in neat brick, the pavilion floor, steps, and edge of the pool unify the yard and give it a clean, crisp look. Inside the pavilion, a spacious seating area accommodates large get-togethers or intimate gatherings.

During the day, light from the sun reflects off the water, but as dusk sets in, lights along the edge of the pool and from within the pavilion give the long pool a magical look. Grass along the brick edge ensures comfort for bare feet.

Comfortable lounge chairs at poolside offer an open sky view that welcomes sunshine or starlight. Climbing vines drape over the columns supporting the house and pavilion, creating a natural transition between the pavilion and pool.

OPPOSITE THE PAVILION AT THE END OF THE POOL IS A PERFECT PLACE TO ESCAPE HARSH RAYS OR SIT AND RELAX LONG AFTER THE SUN HAS SET.

ABOVE SCULPTURES ON THE POOL'S EDGE ADD AN ARTISTIC TOUCH TO THE ENTERTAINING AREA.

Great
Escape

Get away from the hustle and bustle in a sunny, inviting landscape that promises relaxation.

LEFT A COZY SEATING AREA SERVES AS A SPOT FOR ENJOYING AN AFTERNOON SNACK OR JUST RELAXING AND ENJOYING THE WARMTH OF THE SUN.

OPPOSITE BLOOMING GREENERY BY THE POOL ADDS LIFE AND VIBRANCY. A WHITE TILED EDGE SLEEKLY DIVIDES THE POOL AND SPA.

a rock-edged pool and spa, classical furnishings, and vibrant plantings create an enticing getaway in this California backyard.

Low retaining walls made of stones surround the property as well as the pool and convey a natural beauty while visually bringing everything together. A guest house next to the pool and spa offers easy access to a shower, bath, and changing area. It also provides an indoor recreation spot on rainy days and respite from the sun on hot afternoons.

Open-air seating shaded by a colorful umbrella provides an ideal dining area and allows visitors to enjoy the scenery. Wrought-iron furniture topped with comfortable seat cushions allows diners to relax and take in the sounds of a waterfall that flows over a bed of stones and into the pool several feet below. Hanging plants and the unusual shape of the pool add a Mediterranean feel to the landscape.

ABOVE THE GUEST HOUSE NEAR THE POOL AREA DOUBLES AS A POOL HOUSE AND PROVIDES AN INDOOR RECREATION SPOT WHEN SWIMMERS NEED A BREAK FROM THE SUN.

OPPOSITE A WATERFALL CASCADING OVER RUGGED ROCKS LENDS A NATURAL LOOK AND SERENE SOUNDS TO THE LANDSCAPE.

chapter 2
Relax
in an Ahh Spa

Beyond Blue

This luxurious hilltop retreat shows how even a small yard can include a pool and spa.

LEFT Deep cobalt blue tiles make the water seem all the more cool and inviting.

OPPOSITE More deep blue tiles on the bottom of the pool define lanes so that two people can work out and swim laps.

ELEVATING THE SPA AT
THE FAR END OF THE
POOL TAKES ADVANTAGE
OF THE BREATHTAKING
VALLEY VIEW. A SLIVER
OF SPACE POOLSIDE
ACCOMMODATES LOUNGE
CHAIRS FOR A PAIR OF
SUN WORSHIPPERS.

a

A compact hilltop location in Cardiff, California, inspired this lofty design for a mini pool and spa.

Elevating the spa at one end of the 45-foot-long lap pool allows bathers to enjoy the valley view as much as the rolling warm water. A niche in the spa edge allows water to spill over into the lap pool below, which widens to 15 feet so that children have plenty of room to play.

The remainder of the pool features two swimming lanes, stylishly designated by a line of cobalt blue tiles on the bottom. More deep blue tiles surround the spa and border the pool steps.

This retreat offers practical function with defined lanes that provide a good practice setting for children's swim meets. Safety is also at the forefront. Two electronically controlled covers meet at the center of the extra-long pool, and another cover protects children from the spa.

Aloha Oasis

Say hello to a piece of paradise every time you come home: Re-create this backyard spa-and-pool getaway surrounded by tropical beauty.

LEFT Bromeliads form a vibrant crown of tropical color.

OPPOSITE THE POOL IS DESIGNED AS A SERIES OF INTERSECTING CIRCLES; THIS SPILLWAY CONTINUES THE THEME AND ADDS THE SOOTHING SOUND OF CASCADING WATER.

If you love the tropics and are fortunate to live in a mild climate, an exotic escape could be as close as your own backyard. This backyard takes full advantage of the warm San Diego weather by harboring a Hawaiian-inspired sanctuary complete with a lagoonlike pool and spa.

Natural stone decking, a waterfall-curtained grotto, and a lush surrounding garden of tall palm fronds and other tropical greenery transport this landscape to a fantasy paradise. Plantings are so thick that pathways from the pool and spa are sheltered by "tunnels" of foliage that lead to secluded garden "rooms."

Artificial gray-black boulders have been drizzled with copper stain to simulate the oxidizing effect of water, suggesting the lava outcroppings of a tropical island.

The pool itself features a "beach" of slate pavers that provide gently sloping access into the water. The illusion continues across the pool bottom, which is surfaced with an aqua-and-black pebble coating.

All around the interior edges of the pool, underwater benches provide resting places; even the waterfall harbors a hidden bench beyond the curtain of water.

As a playful finishing touch, a fiery orange bromeliad seems to flair like a bonfire from amid an island of stacked stone situated between the spa and pool.

Outdoor lighting ensures that the lagoon continues to be as inviting when the sun sets.

RAISED PLANTING BEDS
BRING TROPICAL GROWTH
RIGHT TO THE WATER'S
EDGE. THE ARTIFICIAL
BOULDER IN THE POOL
SERVES AS A BASKING
PLACED OR STEADIES
BATHERS AS THEY
TRAVERSE THE SLOPING
SLATE "BEACH" INTO THE
LAGOON.

At-Home Holiday

EVERY DAY CAN BE A VACATION GETAWAY WHEN YOU CREATE A RESTFUL RETREAT, COMPLETE WITH A TRANQUIL SPA, IN YOUR BACKYARD.

OPPOSITE LOW-MAINTENANCE GRASSES AND PERENNIALS LEND A SOFTENING EFFECT AROUND THE LAP POOL.

LEFT TUCKING A STATUE INTO TALL GRASSES POOLSIDE ADDS INTEREST AND MYSTERY.

OPPOSITE THE SHADY CONFINES OF THE PERGOLA WELCOME DINERS TO ENJOY THE RELAXING SOUNDS OF WATER FLOWING INTO THE LAP POOL.

RIGHT A WIDE PATIO AROUND THE POOL CREATES A SPACIOUS GATHERING PLACE FOR LARGE PARTIES. MULTIPLE SEATING OPTIONS ALLOW CONVERSATION GROUPINGS TO FORM SPONTANEOUSLY.

When you work hard (and who doesn't these days?), you deserve to play with gusto too. That's why a Palo Alto, California, couple designed this backyard, where they can relax, dine, cook, entertain, exercise, and play. It's a space that meets their needs and lifestyle as precisely as any indoor floor plan.

Their ultimate escape is a bubbling spa, which is elegantly defined by slate coping and a soothing soft-gray interior. To ensure privacy from more active areas within the backyard, the spa is situated behind tall shrubs and an Arts and Crafts-style fence that reflects the style of the house.

Because the couple also enjoy regular exercise, their outdoor living space includes a lap pool. When the lap pool isn't in use, it serves as a lovely reflective feature for the pleasure of poolside diners.

(CONTINUED ON PAGE 74)

To accommodate cooking needs, an outdoor kitchen is located only a few steps away from its indoor counterpart, making it more convenient to transport food, dishes, and cooking utensils from indoors to outside.

Intimate dinners can be served at a tranquil spot at one end of the pool, where a pergola hosts a table and chairs.

For large gatherings, the surrounding expansive patio features multiple seating areas and can easily welcome as many as 30 guests, who can mingle and nibble on snacks around the pool.

INCONSPICUOUSLY TUCKED INTO AN OUTDOOR CORNER, YET ONLY STEPS AWAY FROM THE INDOOR KITCHEN, THE ALFRESCO COOKING AREA FEATURES A GAS GRILL AND SINK.

Grand Classic

A SPLENDID SPA AND POOL SPARKLE IN A SIDE YARD LOCATION AND COMPLEMENT THE HOME'S LOVELY ARCHITECTURE.

OPPOSITE FOUR LIMESTONE COLUMNS ARE A DRAMATIC CULMINATION OF THE POOL DESIGN. SEMIEVERGREEN VINES SOFTEN THE COLUMNS' LINES.

LEFT A LION'S HEAD FOUNTAIN IS A TIMELESS DESIGN ELEMENT FROM GREEK AND ROMAN ARCHITECTURE.

LEFT A WATERFALL FLANKED BY LIONS' HEADS SPILLS WATER FROM THE SPA TO THE POOL BELOW AND BRINGS THE GENTLE SPLASHING SOUNDS TO THE GARDEN.

RIGHT THE SAME CHEROKEE LIMESTONE SURROUNDING THE SPA STACKS UP TO FORM THIS SUBSTANTIAL OUTDOOR FIREPLACE, WHICH IS ALSO ELEGANTLY DISTINGUISHED BY A LION'S HEAD.

*a*lthough spas and pools are made for relaxing, they can contribute a dramatic formal effect. This Atlanta side yard shows how water features with crisp geometry, gracious statuary, and rich natural materials make an unforgettably grand statement.

Curvy lines often communicate a casual atmosphere; this rectangular pool and multisided spa reflect the slightly more formal Italian-style stucco home.

To make a seamless connection between the home and recreation area, color schemes, materials, and shapes used in the garden are repeated in the traditional design of the pool and spa.

(TEXT CONTINUED ON PAGE 82)

Grand Classic

MANUFACTURED TILE
DECKING, WHICH MIMICS
THE LOOK OF NATURAL
STONE, CONTINUES FROM
THE POOL AREA TO THIS
OUTDOOR DINING SPACE.

PAGES 80-81 WATER
FROM THE LION'S HEAD
FOUNTAINS AND THE
WATERFALL NICHE
INTRODUCE THE PLEASING
SOUNDS OF SPLASHING
WATER TO THE SIDE YARD.

Tightly clipped hedges and 20 Leyland cypress trees enhance the reserve effect. The trees also cleverly conceal the code-required pool fence.

Color is kept to a minimum with dark green foliage serving as the backdrop to subtle splashes of pastel flowers.

Rounding out this outdoor retreat are an intimate dining area, poolside chaises for lounging, and a handsome limestone fireplace that can be used to make evening gatherings cozy and inviting.

Ultimate Perch

POSITION A SPA WITH THE BEST SEATS FOR A SPECTACULAR VIEW.

LEFT A FLOATING LOUNGER EXTENDS SEATING OPTIONS INTO THE POOL.

OPPOSITE THE STILL SURFACE OF THE POOL REFLECTS THE SKY, ENHANCING THE TRANQUIL BEAUTY OF THE SETTING.

This spa and pool provide a cool escape from the relentless summer heat. The design takes full advantage of the hillside perch.

Positioned at the highest point of the site, the spa serves as *the* spot for relaxing. Its warm, bubbling waters soothe the body. The spectacular view inspires the mind.

Matching the drama of the distant scenery is the vanishing-edge pool; when viewed from the house it appears to melt into the body of water beyond. In reality, the far wall of the swimming pool is constructed a few inches shorter than the pool's other walls. This way only a little water cascades over the edge, where a basin catches it and recirculates it into the pool.

A granite patio leads up to the edge of the pool, which is rimmed in limestone tiles to match the house.

OPPOSITE A SECOND-LEVEL DECK ON THE BACK OF THE HOUSE PROVIDES SHADE TO ANYONE LOUNGING ON THE GRANITE POOLSIDE PATIO BELOW.

ABOVE SITUATED CLOSE TO THE SPA, THIS DINING SPOT BOASTS A DRAMATIC VIEW.

Aged Perfection

RUSTIC MATERIALS MAKE A NEW SPA APPEAR AS GENTLY AGED AS THE RECENTLY CONSTRUCTED HOUSE.

LEFT ARIZONA FLAGSTONE, PALA ROCK, AND THREE OTHER QUARRY STONES GIVE THE PATIO AND SPA AN OLD-WORLD LOOK.

OPPOSITE RECYCLED MATERIALS ADD TO THE VINTAGE LOOK. WOODEN POSTS SUPPORTING THE VERANDA ROOF, FOR EXAMPLE, WERE ONCE PART OF A FREEWAY OVERPASS.

AGED PERFECTION

THE RETAINING WALLS OF
THE SPA STACK UP FOR
RUSTIC STYLE AND STAND
IN AS EXTRA SEATING.
RED FLAGSTONE PAVERS
FEATURE JOINTS FILLED
WITH CREEPING MINT TO
SOFTEN THE HARDSCAPE
AND LEND COLOR.

Sometimes a sparkling spa suits the surroundings to a T. However, in the case of this newly constructed Southern California residence, which is designed to look like an old Tuscan villa, a spanking new spa and barren landscape would have looked out of place.

Instead of concrete, stucco, or tile—which would have appeared too new—five types of natural stone create a poolside retaining wall. The stacked stone gives the outdoor living space rustic appeal and complements the well-aged appearance of the house.

Plantings with a mature appearance—creeping ficus, scrambling dwarf ivy, and date palms—further enhance the established look, as though the landscape has been this way for ages. Even the gaps between the flagstones are filled with creeping dwarf mint to match the vintage facade.

The illusion continues to the home's exterior where wood beams, once used as forms for shoring up freeway overpasses, serve as sturdy posts for the veranda.

Leisure Rooms

THIS DECK DEFINES THREE ROOMS FOR OUTDOOR ACTIVITIES, INCLUDING A DEDICATED SPACE FOR THE SWIM SPA.

LEFT ONE STEP UP FROM THE ADJOINING DECK, THIS GAZEBO PROVIDES A SHELTERED, SHADY SPOT FOR DINING.

OPPOSITE A BUILT-IN GRILL NESTLES INTO ONE CORNER OF THE SPA DECK FOR CONVENIENT OUTDOOR COOKING.

LEFT STEPS OFF THE CENTER PORTION OF THE DECK PROVIDE ACCESS TO THE BACKYARD AND A PATIO AREA TUCKED BENEATH THE GAZEBO.

RIGHT AMPLE DECKING SURROUNDS THE SWIM SPA, PROVIDING PLACES TO RELAX, CHAT, AND ENJOY A COOL DRINK.

When designed with a good floor plan, a deck can host several outdoor activities simultaneously. Begin your planning by listing all the activities you would like your dream deck and patio to accommodate, then adapt the design accordingly. You can use partitions, level changes, arbors, railings, and other architectural devices to designate specific activity areas.

This Colorado deck features steps and level changes to define three distinct spaces, or "rooms." The lowest level of the deck features a cooking area with a built-in grill. A tiled surface around the grill offers counter space for holding serving plates and utensils. This level also holds an 8×16-foot swim spa.

The deck is large enough to accommodate a clear walkway around the spa as well as comfortable gathering spaces. Allowing sufficient space for all potential functions is key to a successful deck plan. Flanking the center deck are a pair of additional decks, providing more space for mingling or relaxing.

At the uppermost level, the deck features a gazebo that's ideal for dining in the shade. A ceiling fan makes the gazebo even more cool and comfortable on muggy days. When planning your own gazebo, consider the size of the table plus the chairs and allow for plenty of room to walk around the table and to pull out chairs.

Key to Solitude

THINK CREATIVELY AND YOU COULD ENJOY A RETREAT AS PRIVATE AND PERSONAL AS THIS KEYHOLE-SHAPE SPA.

LEFT WATER SPILLING INTO A RESERVOIR OFFERS PLEASING SOUNDS AND REQUIRES LESS MAINTENANCE THAN A POND.

OPPOSITE A VINE-COVERED FENCE AND A GLOSSY-LEAVED MAGNOLIA TREE OFFER PRIVACY AROUND THIS UNUSUAL, STYLISH SPA.

OPPOSITE ONE OF THE SPEAKERS IS VISIBLE IN THE STONE FENCE SUPPORT BESIDE THE SPA, LOCATED A FEW SHORT STEPS DOWN FROM THE COVERED PORCH.

RIGHT A LAMINATED-GLASS ROOF TOPS THE TRELLIS TO PROTECT THIS OUTDOOR KITCHEN FROM THE RAINY VANCOUVER CLIMATE.

Creating backyard privacy for a newly constructed home can be difficult because many building sites lack mature trees and other plantings. This new Vancouver, British Columbia, home conquers the challenge with a large transplanted tree, vines, and a fence to ensure seclusion.

Because a spa, waterfall, and outdoor kitchen are located on a second-story terrace, the space could have been seen by all. Instead, vines were planted to cover the fence, and a stately magnolia tree was installed to help establish privacy and serenity.

(CONTINUED ON PAGE 100)

A STAND-ALONE
WATERFALL PROVIDES
ENOUGH PLEASANT
SOUND TO OBSCURE
STREET NOISE. THE
CONCRETE STRUCTURE IS
ALSO EASY TO CARE FOR.

Adding to the air of tranquility is the soft gray slate patio surrounding the spa, which has an unusual keyhole shape. The spa is located close to the house, so it is likely to be used more often than one located in the far reaches of the yard. The spa becomes more enjoyable thanks to the dining and cooking areas located nearby.

Adding dimension to this outdoor room, hidden speakers are situated near the spa. The speakers can pipe music to the area with a push of a button. On chilly evenings a portable heater can be fired up to make everyone comfortable.

chapter 3
Bring the Inside Out

Backyard Beauty

MAKE OUTDOOR LIVING AS INVITING AS POSSIBLE BY PLANNING YOUR OUTDOOR SPACES AS CAREFULLY AS YOU DO YOUR INTERIORS.

LEFT A POTTING BENCH, BRICK PAVERS, AND A WATER SPIGOT TURN A CORRIDOR BETWEEN THE HOUSE AND GARAGE INTO A PRACTICAL WORKSPACE.

OPPOSITE COLORFUL BLOOMS MAKE THE PATIO DINING AREA INVITING. A WHITE PERGOLA CROWNED WITH TRUMPET VINES DRAWS THE EYE UP TOWARD THE GREEN LANDSCAPE.

OPPOSITE WISTERIA AND A TRICKLING WALL FOUNTAIN MAKE THIS REDWOOD PERGOLA AN ENTICING RETREAT.

RIGHT PERENNIAL PLANTINGS ACCENT THE PATIO NEAR THE GARAGE.

PAGES 108-109 PATIOS AND RAISED BRICK PLANTERS TRANSFORM A BASIC BACKYARD INTO A SERIES OF GATHERING PLACES.

Practical living spaces surrounded by plants and accents in vibrant hues make this California backyard a favorite gathering place.

A brick patio flows seamlessly from the sides and rear of the home as a natural extension of living space. Although designed for outdoor use, the chunky wooden dining table looks as handsome as many indoor tables. Brightly painted ceramic pots filled with colorful annuals bring additional color and style to the dining area. Behind the table, trumpet vines crown a white-painted pergola.

From the patio, broad brick steps descend to a lawn rimmed with bright perennials. Across this expanse, another pergola, this one made of rustic, weathered redwood and capped by wisteria, houses a seating area that's a haven of tranquility. Near the seating area, a trickling stone fountain heightens the sense of serenity. The fountain stone matches the granite found on the front of the home.

Functional Form

DEFINE YOUR LANDSCAPE WITH BEAUTIFUL FOUNTAINS AND EYECATCHING ACCENTS.

LEFT INSET SQUARES OF BLUE-GRAY SLATE AMONG CONCRETE PAVERS CREATE A CRAFTSMAN-ERA FOURSQUARE PATTERN IN THE PATIO.

OPPOSITE A WICKER CHAIR ENCOURAGES RELAXATION UNDER A COOL CANOPY OF LEAVES. THE RIVER ROCK FOUNTAIN ENCASEMENT IS CAPPED WITH HAND-HEWED BASALT STONE.

LEFT THE PERGOLA AND THE ARBOR ABOVE THE FENCE REFLECT CRAFTSMAN DESIGN ELEMENTS FOUND THROUGHOUT THE HOME.

RIGHT THE ARBOR ABOVE THE GATE, THE DOUBLE FOURSQUARE FENCE, AND A MATCHING LANTERN ALL REFLECT TRADITIONAL CRAFTSMAN STYLING.

This low-maintenance courtyard underscores the Craftsman-era mantra: Meld form with function. Time-honored shapes and lines, such as the cutout squares on the fence and the styling of the wooden settee, reflect true Craftsman style.

All construction materials—cedar, river rock, basalt stone, and tumbled concrete pavers—were chosen for their low-maintenance properties. The hefty proportions on the fence posts, pergola columns, and stonework also convey a sense of handcrafted permanence.

Planned open space gives the garden an air of serenity. Rather than crowding the area with plants and furniture, the design includes furnishings that are few but well-chosen.

Variations from typical Craftsman styling, a fountain and comfy wicker chairs lend comfort to the space.

When the shade from the trees is not enough, guests can pop open the colorful umbrella above the table area. Evergreens, bulbs, and perennials provide low-maintenance greenery.

ABOVE REFLECTING THE SAME ATTENTION TO DETAIL AS THE REST OF THE GARDEN, THE ENCLOSURE FOR THE GARBAGE CANS ADDS A TOUCH OF ELEGANCE TO A UTILITARIAN AREA.

RIGHT BUILDERS CAREFULLY WORKED THE NEW COURTYARD AROUND EXISTING VEGETATION. THE RESULT IS RELIEF FROM THE SUN IN THE SHADE OF MATURE TREES.

Spanish Spice

A DARING COLOR PALETTE AND A THOUGHTFUL LANDSCAPE DESIGN DEFINE THIS SPANISH-STYLE COURTYARD.

LEFT ARTWORK DECORATES THE BACK SIDE OF THE COURTYARD BANQUETTE AND PROVIDES A GLIMPSE OF THE COLOR SCHEME USED IN THE INTERIOR OF THE HOME.

OPPOSITE STRATEGICALLY PLACED STUCCO WALLS PERFORM DOUBLE DUTY HERE: LOW-PROFILE ACCENT WALLS BOLDLY DEFINE OUTDOOR ROOMS WHILE TALLER, STREET-SHIELDING WALLS AFFORD PRIVACY.

OPPOSITE THIS LARGE C-SHAPE WALL CARRIES A THIRD ROLE AS A STYLISH BANQUETTE. CUSHIONS MADE OF FABRIC INSPIRED BY SPANISH TILES ADD A TOUCH OF COMFORT TO THE STONE SEAT.

RIGHT ON THE OPPOSITE SIDE OF THE YARD, DESERT-LIKE PLANTS, SUCH AS THIS AGAVE, TAKE CENTER STAGE.

The Spanish-inspired architectural features of this Southern California home served as the inspiration for a colorful outdoor living space. A large expanse of stone underfoot and built-in stucco features placed in the landscape complement the home's adobe-style walls.

Colorful built-in stone seating and painted walls strike a balance between a south-of-the border gallery and a plant lover's paradise. Large, architectural art is prominently displayed on the colorfully painted stucco walls while a quiet range of blue, silver, and bronze plant foliage softens the vibrant color.

A fountain reminiscent of those found in Spanish missions adds the soothing sounds of flowing water to the cheerful outdoor retreat.

Multilevel Menagerie

Transform a compact backyard into a three-tiered living space.

LEFT A WALL-MOUNTED UMBRELLA GIVES ADDITIONAL FLEXIBILITY IN SHIELDING GUESTS FROM SUN OR AN UNEXPECTED SHOWER.

OPPOSITE GARDEN-STYLE LATTICE PANELS COMBINE WITH CHEERFUL YELLOW STUCCO WALLS TO ENCLOSE THE SLATE-TILED COURTYARD IN STYLE.

OPPOSITE

ARCHITECTURAL DETAILS,
SUCH AS CROWN MOLDING
AND WALL SCONCES,
MAKE THE COURTYARD AS
STYLISH AS ANY
INTERIOR SPACE.

RIGHT BUILT-IN
SPEAKERS AND WALL-
MOUNTED LAMPS MAKE
ENTERTAINING EASY, BOTH
DAY AND NIGHT.

The space limitations of an urban setting can make comfortable outdoor living a challenge to achieve. This tiny backyard of a Chicago graystone was transformed into a tropical garden oasis by building up instead of out.

The main level is a 16×16-foot deck built atop the garage and level with the family room and kitchen. A corkscrew stairway leads to the second level, a 16×25-foot deck that can also be reached from the study. Access to the private upper balcony, which is also the ceiling for the second deck, is obtained through the top-floor master bedroom.

Upbeat colors and textures, such as yellow stucco and green crown molding, make for a lively surround. Wood lattice and open-design ironwork let light and fresh air filter through the spaces. Built-in benches keep the main level from appearing cluttered and provide seating for a crowd. A glass-top table all but disappears, giving the illusion of more open space.

(CONTINUED ON PAGE 124)

LEFT UNDER THE EAVES OF THE UPPER BALCONY, THE OUTDOOR LIVING ROOM IS PROTECTED FROM THE ELEMENTS. WROUGHT-IRON GATES OFFER SECURITY, ARE DECORATIVE, AND ALLOW MORE AIR TO FLOW.

OPPOSITE A COMBINATION OF COVERED AND UNCOVERED LIVING SPACE LETS THE ENTERTAINING CONTINUE RAIN OR SHINE.

On hot days, a fan attached to a cantilevered beam stirs up a cool breeze. Chilly nights are made more comfortable with the help of a built-in fireplace.

A combination of tropical plants—including palms, hibiscus, and elephant's ear—fill the numerous planter boxes and movable containers that surround the living space and hide nearby buildings from view. A fountain helps muffle street noise.

Private Paradise

ENSURE SOME PEACE AND QUIET WITH A SERIES OF NEW GARDEN ROOMS.

LEFT GARDEN STATUARY
GIVES THE OUTDOOR
ROOMS THE SAME
SENSE OF STYLE FOUND IN
INDOOR ROOMS.

OPPOSITE MADE
FROM WATERPROOF
POLYPROPYLENE,
THIS SOFA AND CHAIR
CAN BE LEFT OUTSIDE
FOR ALL FOUR OF
COLORADO'S SEASONS.
THE FURNISHINGS ARE
LOCATED JUST OUTSIDE
THE HOME'S OFFICE AREA
AND PROVIDE A COMFY
PLACE TO GATHER FOR
CASUAL MEETINGS.

OPPOSITE A NEW CEDAR TRELLIS SHADES THE COURTYARD DINING ROOM, AND A CUSTOM GRANITE TABLE OFFERS SEATING FOR EIGHT.

RIGHT A BRIDGE WITH STAINLESS-STEEL RAILING SPANS THE FOUNTAIN AND A WATERFALL-LIKE SPILLWAY NEAR THE COURTYARD'S ENTRY DOOR.

PAGES 130-131 SEVERAL STEPS UP FROM THE FOUNTAIN ENTRY IS THE BREAKFAST PATIO AND THE ORIGINAL, NOW TOTALLY PRIVATE ENTRANCE TO THE HOUSE. HARDY PORCELAIN TILES EDGED WITH SANDSTONE PAVERS MAKE UP THE NEW PATIO FLOOR.

Even if you live on a busy city street, you can create outdoor comfort. This Denver home, located on a major thoroughfare, lacked any outdoor privacy, and the constant traffic made playing outside unsafe for small children. Adding walled courtyards between the house and the detached garage and in the backyard solves both privacy and safety issues and reduces traffic noise.

An oak entry door leads from the front drive to the first garden room where sounds of a waterfall further disguise the noise of the traffic beyond.

Inside the entry door, a flight of steps leads to a sunny whitewashed patio that includes an outdoor living area complete with sofas, chairs, and a dining center. Additional furnishings occupy the patio outside the home office, providing comfortable seating and work space for casual business meetings.

Hillside Haven

TRANSFORM A SLOPED YARD INTO AN OUTDOOR PARADISE WITH MEANDERING PATHS, A PRIVATE PATIO, AND A PRETTY PERGOLA.

LEFT WROUGHT-IRON FURNISHINGS ADD DESIGN DASH TO THE PATIO.

OPPOSITE LOW-GROWING SHRUBS, PERENNIAL ORNAMENTAL GRASSES, AND A THICK LAYER OF MULCH HOLD THE SLOPING SOIL IN PLACE. AT THE TOP OF THE STAIRS, A WROUGHT-IRON ARBOR FRAMES A VIEW OF SEVERAL PERENNIAL FLOWER BEDS.

Step into this stylish backyard garden, and you'd never guess that the area was once nothing more than a steep patch of barren ground beside an unpleasantly public terrace. A few clever changes make the space inviting, functional, and private.

Stone steps create a graceful ascent to a new paver-covered area created by leveling an additional 15 square feet of ground. A combination of open-air patio, a shaded pergola, and a dining pavilion make the patio comfortable and usable rain or shine. Concrete pavers cover the once bare ground and require little maintenance. An automatic irrigation system makes ensures that watering the plants is never a chore; an automatic timer controls the landscape lighting system.

The backyard slopes toward the house, so neighbors could easily peer from their higher perch directly into the yard. However, a neighborhood association rule limited the fence height to 6 feet. To solve the problem, a privacy fence was placed 4 feet up the slope from the patio, creating the equivalent of a 12-foot-high fence.

OPPOSITE A ROOF CONSTRUCTED OF TRANSPARENT PANELS ALLOWS PLENTY OF LIGHT IN YET STILL PROTECTS DINERS FROM INCLEMENT WEATHER.

ABOVE A NEW SHED MAKES POTTING FLOWERS EASY. THE SHED IS EQUIPPED WITH ELECTRICITY, RUNNING WATER, A GREENHOUSE WINDOW, AND A WIDE DOOR FOR MOVING EQUIPMENT IN AND OUT.

HILLSIDE HAVEN

PAGES 136-137
A SUBDUED COLOR
PALETTE FOR THE
FOUNTAIN, BENCH, SHED,
PERGOLA, AND PATIO
ENSURES THE COLORFUL
FLOWERS AND FOLIAGE
TAKE CENTER STAGE.

RIGHT WISTERIA VINES
SOFTEN THE LOOK OF
THE PERGOLA'S LOAD-
BEARING POSTS.

OPPOSITE CEDAR
BOARDS ATOP PRESSURE-
TREATED POSTS FORM
A STYLISH PERGOLA
OVER A COMFORTABLE
SEATING AREA. LAYERS OF
ANNUALS, PERENNIALS,
VINES, SHRUBS, AND
HANGING BASKETS STAND
OUT AGAINST THE MELLOW
EARTHTONES OF THE
WOOD STRUCTURES.

Gated Garden

EVEN IF YOU LIVE ON A BUSY STREET CORNER, YOUR BACKYARD CAN BECOME A PRIVATE SANCTUARY.

LEFT CLAY POTS FILLED WITH BRIGHTLY COLORED FLOWERS ADD COLOR AND LIFE TO THE GARDEN ROOMS.

OPPOSITE A SPANISH-STYLE DOOR IN THE GARDEN WALL LEADS TO A PATIO BRIGHTENED BY LUSH TROPICAL PLANTS.

LEFT LUSH PALMS AND A THREE-TIERED FOUNTAIN ADD TO THE OPEN-AIR AMBIENCE. WOODEN LOVE SEATS AND A COFFEE TABLE PROVIDE LIVING ROOM COMFORT.

ABOVE WHETHER YOU PREFER FRESH AIR COMBINED WITH SUNSHINE OR SHADE, THIS PATIO HAS WHAT YOU NEED. A COMBINATION OF CUSHY FURNISHINGS, POTTED PLANTS, AND OUTDOOR STATUARY GIVE THE GARDEN SPACE A SENSE OF STYLE.

Establishing privacy for a patio located on a busy street corner can pose a challenge, especially when your home sits on a street corner open to traffic on two sides. This Southwestern-style landscape solves the problem through innovative design.

Adding tall stucco walls blocks the view to and from adjoining streets. The light, cheerful yellow wall color reflects sunshine and provides a pleasant backdrop for furniture, plants, and artwork. The stucco matches the walls of the home so closely that from the front, it's difficult to discern where the interior stops and the exterior begins. New French doors open to enticing views of the garden and can be left open in good weather.

(CONTINUED ON PAGE 146)

Innovative design details give this patio a Mediterranean feel. Here, a stucco wall topped with roof tile extends the home's architecture into the garden.

LEFT THIS SIMPLE TILE FOUNTAIN HELPS DROWN OUT THE SOUND OF TRAFFIC AND CREATE A MORE PEACEFUL FEELING.

RIGHT STATUARY, AN ARCHED DOOR, AND PAINTED STUCCO WALLS MAKE THIS OUTDOOR SPACE FEEL MUCH LIKE AN INTERIOR ROOM.

Large, square paving stones surrounded by creeping plants create a low-maintenance walkway. An airy pergola attached to the house provides relief from the sun.

A clear view of the sky, splashed with the greenery of tall trees and shrubs, lends an open feeling, even though the area is walled in. Giant banana trees, colorful cannas plants, and saltillo tiles maintain the Southwestern theme through each of the garden rooms.

chapter 4

Find Serenity
with Water

Asian Tranquillity

SERENITY, TRANQUILLITY, AND MEDITATION ARE ALL ATTAINABLE WHEN YOU TURN TO A LITTLE FLAVOR FROM THE EAST.

LEFT A STONE LANTERN AND TRADITIONAL BAMBOO FENCING HELP SET THE THEME FOR AN ASIAN LANDSCAPE AND ARE IDEAL COMPANIONS TO ANY STREAMS OR POOLS WITHIN THE GARDEN.

OPPOSITE THIS TRADITIONAL BAMBOO WATERSPOUT WITH A STONE BASIN PROVIDES THE SOUND OF RUNNING WATER, ADDING SERENITY AND CREATING A PLACE FOR MEDITATION.

Japanese landscapes are prized for their calm atmosphere. But if you thought you had to have raked gravel and a forest of bamboo to create your own Eastern-influenced garden, consider this more subtle approach that can suit most any neighborhood.

Asian-inspired architecture, a soothing water feature, and an air of simplicity are at the heart of the look and feel you desire. Gateways and fences offer an opportunity to introduce elements that reflect Japanese style. Small bridges with less-prominent arches—rather than the more traditional half-moon bend—can add to the effect. Without going overboard, a small stone lantern or two can blend into the landscape.

(CONTINUED ON PAGE 154)

LEFT USING A GENTLE ARCH RATHER THAN A FULL HALF-MOON SHAPE FOR THIS BRIDGE ENABLES IT TO KEEP THE GARDEN FOCUSED AROUND THE SOFTLY FLOWING WATER WHILE STILL EVOKING THE JAPANESE THEME.

ABOVE THE BUBBLING SPA IS AN IDEAL PLACE TO ENJOY THE TRANQUILLITY OF THE GARDEN. A BAMBOO FENCE AND WELL-PLACED BOULDERS BRING IN THE ELEMENTS OF ASIAN STYLE.

LEFT The decorative entryway into the garden announces to visitors they are about to set foot in a retreat infused with Eastern tranquillity.

RIGHT A small stream running through this landscape exudes a Japanese aura and offers the garden a dreamlike atmosphere.

Hiding these Asian elements behind a high wall will allow the garden to feel like a sanctuary and help whisk away stress. A bamboo fence adds to the Eastern feel while providing privacy for a spa.

Water is a must-have feature for an Asian garden. A small pool in the hollow of a large rock with a traditional bamboo waterspout will add a calming and comfortable sound to the garden. This garden also features a meandering stream that provides numerous places for quiet reflection.

Tropical Paradise

You might not live in Hawaii, but you can still recreate much of this exotic water-filled wonderland in your own backyard.

LEFT A JAPANESE WATER BASIN SERVES AS A REFLECTING POOL AND COMPLEMENTS THE GREENERY THAT SURROUNDS IT.

OPPOSITE ADDING A POND NEAR A PORCH LETS YOU ENJOY EVERYTHING ABOUT HAVING WATER IN YOUR GARDEN WITHOUT EVER HAVING TO LEAVE YOUR CHAIR.

Combining water with a tropical theme can create dreamlike results for any garden, even if you live in a less-than-tropical climate. Portable plants and smart substitutions make this vacationlike scenario possible.

This lovely landscape—complete with a lily-filled pond—is in Hawaii, but hardy varieties of water plants and a pond dug below the frost line make it possible to winter over many water plants in a cold northern climate.

You can even have the tropical plants. The secret is to make them moveable and effortless for storing when that first frost comes. Place them in containers that can be easily transported. Set the containers around the pond and even sink a few below ground level for a more integrated appearance. Before cold weather arrives, transfer the potted plants to inside the house—and enjoy your tropical garden all winter long.

Many indoor tropical plants thrive outdoors during the summer if given the right shade to protect them from the sun. Schefflera, mother-in-law's tongue, and spider plants are a few of those that flourish. Bamboo and tall grasses are also ideal for creating a more tropical atmosphere and will produce a lush backdrop for all your yard's water features.

ABOVE POLYNESIAN-STYLE ACCENTS, SUCH AS THE BAMBOO TORCHES, ENHANCE THE TROPICAL FLAIR OF THIS GARDEN.

OPPOSITE YOU MAY NOT BE ABLE TO HAVE TALL PALMS, BUT SHORTER VARIETIES CAN BE POTTED AND PLACED AROUND THE LANDSCAPE. MOVE THEM TO A SHELTERED PLACE WHEN YOU CLOSE THE POOL FOR THE SEASON.

TROPICAL PARADISE

An organic shape makes this swimming pool look like a naturally occurring body of water. Rocks and greenery surrounding the pool enhance the relaxed, natural feel without interfering with the benefits of swimming.

Abundant Water

FROM TRANQUIL PONDS TO TRICKLING STREAMS, WATER TREATMENTS CAN BEAUTIFY ANY OUTDOOR AREA.

LEFT A SIMPLE WOODEN BENCH ALONG THE STONE PATH IS A NICE PLACE TO SIT AND LISTEN TO THE FLOW OF THE STREAM OR GAZE AT THE COLORFUL SURROUNDINGS.

OPPOSITE THE SMALL WATERFALL NEAR THE TOP OF THIS GARDEN CIRCULATES THE SOUND OF RUNNING WATER THROUGHOUT THE AREA.

Even if you have a yard that is flat-as-a-pancake—as this one once was—you can plan ponds and streams that yield interesting topography and unforgettable character.

Eighty tons of rock helped shape this water-filled wonderland. Rocks of various sizes and leftover soil from digging two ponds and a stream made dramatic elevation changes possible, including a focal point 3-foot-drop waterfall. Colorful plantings and dwarf trees placed near the still water give off double the amount of color as they are reflected off quiet ponds.

A cascading stream cuts the landscape in two and a stone path winds its way through the now-contoured backyard. Benches and boulders provide resting places to enjoy the vast details and plantings and to listen to the trickling water. A small deck provides yet another view point of this project.

ABOVE A STONE PATH COMPLEMENTS THE STREAMING WATER, ENCOURAGING STROLLS THROUGH THE MAGNIFICENT BACKYARD.

OPPOSITE ROCK AND SOIL LEFT OVER FROM DIGGING PONDS AND STREAMS ENABLED ELEVATION CHANGES. MOST NOTABLE HERE IS THE 3-FOOT DROP FOR A WATERFALL.

A GENTLE STREAM FLOWS
THROUGH THE TOP OF
THE GARDEN, LEADING
TO A QUIET POND AT THE
BOTTOM. A JAPANESE
MAPLE WITH A CARPET OF
LEMON THYME PROVIDES
DEFINITION AND BEAUTY.
OTHER GREENERY
THAT LIVENS UP THE
GARDEN INCLUDES A
LOW-GROWING CONIFER,
FOXGLOVES, ROSES,
AND ANOTHER BRONZE
JAPANESE MAPLE.

Natural Incline

STAY COOL ON A HOT SUMMER DAY WITH A PONDLIKE SWIMMING POOL AND SERENE WATERFALL.

LEFT A DINING AREA OPPOSITE THE WATERFALL PRESENTS AN ENTICING RETREAT FOR ENJOYING SNACKS OR A RELAXING MEAL AFTER A LONG DAY.

OPPOSITE THE WATERFALL PROVIDES AN AREA TO ENJOY BEING IMMERSED IN WATER. STEPS NEXT TO THE FLOWING WATER OFFER AN ALTERNATIVE WAY TO ENJOY THE COOLING WATER WITHOUT GETTING SOAKED.

RIGHT A WATERFALL IN THE CORNER OF THE POOL, ALONG WITH THE BOULDERS AND GREENERY SURROUNDING IT, GIVES THE WATER A NATURAL AND REFRESHING LOOK.

LEFT BOULDERS ENHANCED WITH FLOWERS AND SHRUBS CREATE A FLAWLESS TRANSITION BETWEEN THE HOUSE AND THE POOL AND COMPLETE THE NATURAL LOOK.

You can enjoy all the fun of a swimming pool—plenty of room to splash and play as well as enough length for swimming laps—without disrupting the beauty that mother nature already brings to your yard. The key is to design the water feature so it looks as though it has always been a part of the surrounding landscape.

This water playground has it all—a slide, a waterfall, and a spa—so no leisure sacrifices were made. But its organic shape and strategically placed boulders around the pool create a natural transition. Enhancing the evolution from artificial to natural are plantings that seem to grow right up to the pool's edge. The greenery adds color and helps soften all the hard edges. Pavers near the water provide a safe walking path but are spaced so that grass fills the gap.

A waterslide could have easily disrupted this illusion. Instead a large outcropping of rocks serves as a clever natural screen and ensures that this swimming pool offers something for everyone.

Mediterranean
Mission

PUT TOGETHER A BOLD
MEDITERRANEAN LOOK AND USE
A WATER FEATURE TO GIVE THE
LANDSCAPE EXTRA DRAMA.

LEFT COLORFUL
SUCCULENTS IN A TERRA-
COTTA POT COMPLEMENT
THE BLUE-TILED FOUNTAIN
SHOWN ON PAGE 174.

OPPOSITE THE STUCCO
WALLS AND CURVED DOOR
ADD TO THE AMBIENCE
AND CREATE A QUIET
ENCLOSURE
SURROUNDED BY FRESH
GREENERY AND FLOWERS.

MEDITERRANEAN MISSION

Imagine a villa garden on the Mediterranean coast of Spain—lush greenery, earthy terra-cotta combined with colored ceramic tiles, and the sounds of a splashing waterfall. This sunny paradise is something you can bring to your own backyard, as this delightful retreat shows.

The elegant clay-tile patio is built all around a spectacular fountain to accommodate an intimate dining table for two and wrought-iron seating.

Stately evergreens and a stucco wall, which is painted terra-cotta, enhance the sense that this is a private seaside escape. The greenery also provides sun control. Terra-cotta pots play up the theme, and the plants they contain help soften the look of the hardscape while bringing splashes of color to the sun-washed patio.

A wide ledge around the water feature can serve as additional seating during parties. For more casual affairs, guests can take off their shoes and swing around to plunge feet and legs into the cool water. In lieu of a pool party, the water feature also doubles as a spa that can accommodate up to 20 people.

Hip Squares

SQUARES CAN CREATE TRANQUIL QUARTERS WHEN CENTERED AROUND A SMALL WATER GARDEN.

OPPOSITE SCULPTURAL CUBES PLAY UP THE CHECKERBOARD DESIGN IN THE FRONT YARD GARDEN. THE WHITE AND GREEN COLOR SCHEME GIVES THE GARDEN A FORMAL LOOK.

LEFT SETTING THE PAVERS FLUSH WITH THE GROUND ALLOWS A MOWER TO PASS OVER WITHOUT INTERRUPTION.

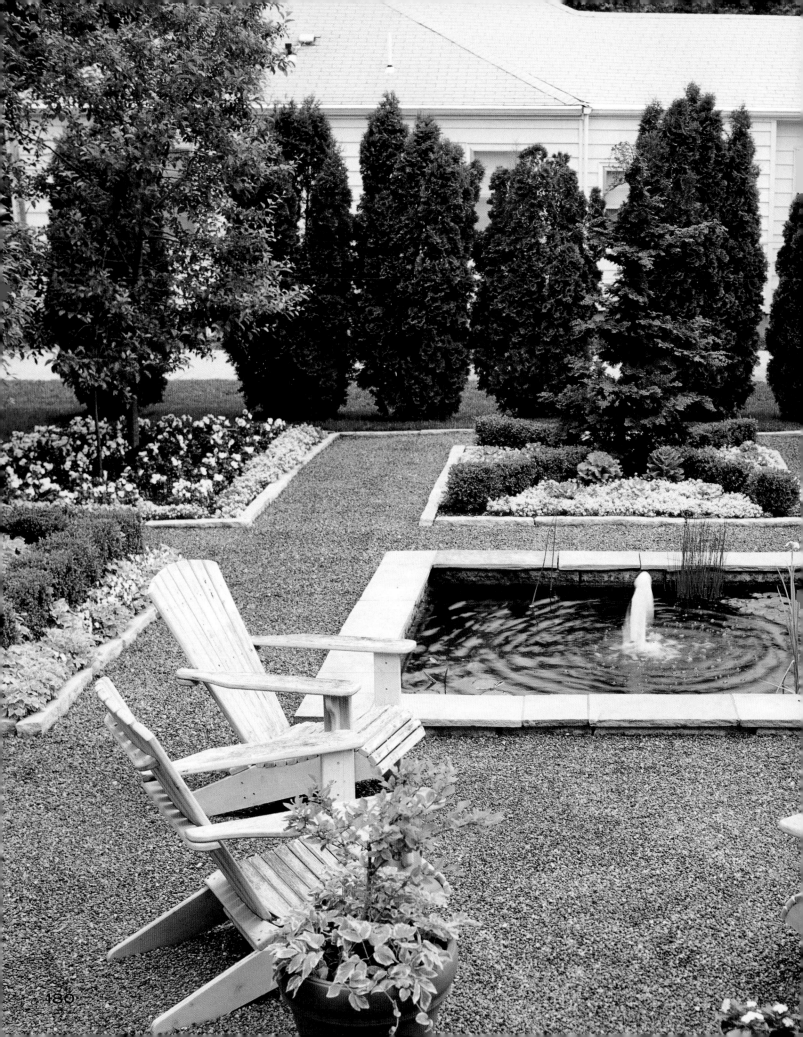

THE WATER GARDEN IN THE CENTER OF THE BACKYARD SERVES AS THE HUB. THE GRAVEL PATHS CONNECT EACH SQUARE TO THE OTHER AND PROVIDE A PLACE FOR ARRANGING A FEW GARDEN CHAIRS.

When casual grace is the order of the day, look to this orderly, formal design to bring quiet beauty to your yard. The secret is to organize your landscape using crisp squares. This garden lays out the geometry horizontally to create a checkerboard that radiates simple elegance. Eight squares are separated by gravel paths to make up the checkerboard façade in the front garden, with the porch acting as the ninth square.

In the backyard, six squares are used, with a water garden and spray making up the front and center square.

A few chairs and plants are placed in the back to allow for a relaxing afternoon or evening listening to the calming water. To maintain the air of formal simplicity, colors are limited to only white and green. Daffodils, white-bud trees, snow-white peonies, pale daylilies, Japanese anemones, annual pansies, alyssum, vinca, and silver-edge ornamental kale fill the beds with white and green.

Crabapple and pine trees complete the setting and lend more depth. (CONTINUED ON PAGE 182)

It's not the size of the lot that counts, but the character it contains. This tiny city lot demonstrates one way to use every square inch to shape an urban oasis.

A bubbling, raised pond in the center of the courtyard is the focus of the area. The bubbling water creates a relaxing sound to ebb away any tension; falling water is also an excellent device for masking city sounds.

Tall grasses at the edge of the water provide texture and greenery to liven up the area. Benches border the perimeter to provide a peaceful place to sit and relax after a long day.

As a finishing touch, climbing plants such as English ivy and climbing hydrangea cover the courtyard with refreshing color and texture.

OPPOSITE GREEN PLANTS SURROUND THE PATIO FOR A COOLING SENSE OF ENCLOSURE AND A HANDSOME CONTRAST TO THE SLATE STONE PATIO.

OPPOSITE THE BUBBLING POND PROVIDES A BACKDROP FOR MORE PLANTINGS. EXTENDING THE POND TWO FEET INTO THE GROUND ENSURES THAT IT DOES NOT FREEZE DURING THE WINTER.

chapter 5
Cozy Up
to the Fire

Natural Wonders

BRING THE ELEMENTS OF NATURE TOGETHER—WATER, FIRE, EARTH, AND SKY—IN A SOUL-SOOTHING SPA.

OPPOSITE THE HAMMERED-METAL FIRE PIT CREATES LIGHT, WARMTH, AND AN INVITING ATMOSPHERE.

LEFT LIGHT-COLOR HEAVILY TEXTURED STEPPING STONES CONTRAST WITH THE DARK AND SMOOTH HOT TUB SURFACES.

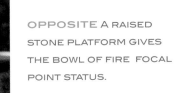

OPPOSITE A RAISED STONE PLATFORM GIVES THE BOWL OF FIRE FOCAL POINT STATUS.

RIGHT THE ROUNDED CURVE OF THE STONE FOUNTAIN CONTRASTS WITH THE RECTANGULAR STEPPINGSTONES AND THE STRONG LINES OF THE SPA.

PAGES 190-191 WATER CASCADES OVER THE EDGE OF THE SPA, FLOWING TO A SURGE TANK HIDDEN UNDER A DECORATIVE PEDESTAL. LOW-MAINTENANCE PLANTS SEAMLESSLY INTEGRATE THE SPACE INTO THE LANDSCAPE.

Bring the elements of nature together—water, fire, earth, and sky—in a soul-soothing spa. To plan your outdoor retreat, study the backyard from both inside and outside the home and settle on a location for the fire pit and spa that will provide views from the house and easy access to a nearby deck and patio.

For this area, the focus is a stunning, inground 9×9-foot spa, its exterior surface adorned in sleek black granite. The design is one of complementary contrasts, where the soothing sounds of water unite with the comforts of fire and light. When the jets are quiet, the spa resumes a tranquil, mirrorlike surface.

Antique Chinese mortar stone forms the bowl of the fountain, with a quiet bubbler spilling over cobblestones. The fire pit consists of a rustic hand-hammered metal bowl, an integrated gas fire ring, and lava rocks.

When the fire is lit, the reflective quality of the fire bowl is enhanced, mirroring the flickering flames. The mirrorlike effects of this water feature are heightened by lining the spa and the shallow reflecting pool in black. The resulting reflection of the sky often gives the illusion of wide open space.

Warm Gatherings

WHAT COULD BE MORE INVITING THAN VISITING, DINING, OR RELAXING AROUND A FLICKERING FIRE?

LEFT SINK-IN SOFT SEATING PROVIDES A COMFORTABLE PLACE FOR EVENING CONVERSATIONS BESIDE THE FIRE.

OPPOSITE THE STONE FIRE PIT GIVES A PLAIN PATIO PURPOSE, SERVING AS THE HUB OF OUTDOOR PARTIES OR INTIMATE EVENINGS FOR TWO.

Inside the house, partygoers always want to gather in the kitchen. But add a fire pit to your patio, and it's sure to become the big draw.

This built-in fire pit, which is made of stone to emphasize the "campfire" connection, becomes a glowing anchor for a conversation grouping of comfortable, cushioned wicker chairs. The round shape is ideal for accommodating intimate or large groups to congregate for conversation and s'mores.

The deck a few steps up from the patio provides more space to accommodate more guests—even the wide steps can double as seating; theater-style lighting on each stair riser lets the party continue well into the night.

Set into one corner of the deck, the screened-in gazebo offers a comfortable place to escape the summer bugs and enjoy a relaxing evening.

(CONTINUED ON PAGE 196)

ABOVE THE GAZEBO, DECK, PATIO, AND HOUSE ARE ALL BROUGHT TOGETHER USING A LOW, OPEN RAILING, MAKING IT HARD TO DISTINGUISH WHERE THE DECK ENDS AND THE HOUSE BEGINS.

OPPOSITE IMAGINE AN EVENING THAT BEGINS WITH DINNER ON THE DECK AND ENDS WITH CONVERSATION, DESSERT, AND DRINKS AROUND THE WARMING FIRE.

When you look out the windows of your house, do you see a backyard that lures you outside? If not, consider carrying the same features, materials, and decorating ideas that you love inside to make the outside just as personal and enticing.

Like any room, the patio needs a focal point, and a fireplace can serve the purpose with panache. This poolside patio, which is outside an old world-style home, features a stucco fireplace with a venerable limestone mantel and flanking wrought-iron faced niches—all of which host the warm glow of candles that augment the fire.

Large wrought-iron candleholders accent the firebox and add even more of a warm glow to the surroundings. Wrought-iron chairs continue the theme and are adorned with cozy cushions covered in outdoor fabrics for comfort and color.

ABOVE FRENCH DOORS LINING THE LOWER LEVEL OF THE HOME MAKE FOR EASY ACCESS TO THE POOL AND PATIOS AND ALLOW FOR A GREAT VIEW FROM INSIDE THE HOME.

OPPOSITE THIS BUILT-IN FIREPLACE SERVES AS A DYNAMIC CENTERPIECE FOR THE PATIO, GIVING OFF A WARM GLOW TO LIGHT THE SEATING AREA AND MAKING GUESTS FEEL RELAXED AND COMFORTABLE.

Southwest Sizzle

AN OUTDOOR FIREPLACE CAN ENHANCE ANY HOME WITH A SOUTHWESTERN SOUL.

LEFT AN OPENING IN THE FIREPLACE WALL PREVENTS THE FEATURE FROM FEELING TOO IMPOSING AND PROVIDES A MEANS FOR SPOTTING ANYONE APPROACHING THE PATIO.

OPPOSITE THE MASSIVE HEARTH BUILT AROUND THIS RELATIVELY SMALL FIREPLACE IS ABLE TO RETAIN THE SIMPLICITY OF PUEBLO DESIGN. THE FIREBOX CAN HOUSE CANDLES OR A FIRE.

SOUTHWEST SIZZLE

ELIMINATING THE HEARTH
LETS THIS SCALED-DOWN
FIREPLACE, WHICH IS CUT
INTO AN EXTERIOR WALL
OF THE HOUSE, FIT IN A
SMALL SPACE.

Your outdoor fireplace doesn't have to be massive to impress. These three homes gained a beautiful yet functional fireplace for the patio while complementing the Southwestern architecture of the home.

The Pueblo-style fireplace on the preceding pages is built into an adobe wall that's constructed to match the height of the home; the firebox is small compared to many. Gorgeous ochre color for the adobe, a subtle shapely design for the fireplace, and a hearth that stretches the width of the wall make it seem like a grand addition. A small window cut into the wall and a pair of sconces lend additional dimension to the area. A log trellis tops off the flagstone patio, finishing the area with appropriate styling.

Less grand, but no less lovely, is the small arched firebox shown here. Raising the feature to eye level makes it a focal point for the entire patio.

(CONTINUED ON PAGE 202)

201

SOUTHWEST SIZZLE

LEFT WROUGHT-IRON FURNISHINGS SUIT THE DESERT STYLING AND PROVIDE A PLACE TO DINE AND RELAX BESIDE THE FIREPLACE.

OPPOSITE TILE INSETS AT THE CORNER OF THE FIREPLACE ADD COLOR AND SOUTHWESTERN STYLE TO THE SURROUND.

For this patio and fireplace, concrete blocks stack up for style and fun. The sandstone patio gained Southwestern personality when courtyard walls were constructed of concrete block and then covered in stucco.

A fireplace is built into the wall, which is whitewashed to reflect the sun and to communicate a clean, uncomplicated look. A window cut into the wall gives a glimpse of plantings beyond—functioning like natural framed artwork for the patio. The cutout also serves a practical purpose, allowing anyone on the patio to see approaching guests.

Terra-cotta flower-filled pots bring color along the top of the wall while a fire burning in the fireplace creates a warm glow—even during the day. Votive candles line the top of the wall as well and can be lit to provide an additional glow to the area during the evening.

Tables and chairs, surrounded by a profusion of bougainvillea, complete the transformation and provide a place for alfresco dining. A rustic wooden table plays up the Southwestern theme and stands ready to serve a buffet or dessert and wine.

Craftsman Charm

DRAMATIC DETAILS LINK THIS OUTDOOR LIVING ROOM AND FIREPLACE TO THE STYLE OF THE HOUSE.

LEFT Flared brick pillars speak clearly to the Craftsman style.

OPPOSITE Bent-willow furnishings continue the rustic appeal of Craftsman styling, as do the grilles on the fireplace doors.

OPPOSITE THE TWO-WAY FIREPLACE ENCOURAGES MAXIMUM OUTDOOR EFFICIENCY BY DEFINING TWO ACTIVITY AREAS: A DINING SPOT ON ONE SIDE AND SEATING AND A SPA ON THE OPPOSITE SIDE.

RIGHT THE MASONRY COLUMNS SUPPORT A TRELLIS TOP THAT DEFINES ONE SIDE OF THE PATIO, PROVIDING SHADE AND BEAUTY.

BELOW AN ELEGANTLY CRAFTED PRIVACY SCREEN LETS GUESTS FEEL COMFORTABLE IN THE SPA AND PROVIDES A CHANGING AREA CLOSE TO THE HOUSE.

An ordinary builder's deck would have been a jarring addition to this handsome Arts and Crafts-style home. Instead the new deck and patios take design cues from the house to make a beautiful transition from indoors to outside.

Craftsman design commonly employs masonry, stone, and wood, so they're natural choices for creating a fitting outdoor living space. Rafters under the eaves of the house are typically exposed, so the same strategy works here with a deck showcasing rafter ends in the eaves of the pergola. Masonry columns feature traditional flared bases, and the two-sided fireplace follows suit.

Rustic limestone lends character to the patio on one side of the fireplace, while dyed concrete provides a durable surface on the opposite side without appearing out of place.

Trimwork in the Craftsman style is usually unadorned, as it is here on the smooth limestone supports and caps on the stairs, the straight-line brickwork, and decorative keyhole cutouts in the privacy screen.

Sinking the modern spa into a surrounding deck of slatted cedar eases the modern feature into the theme.

Year-Round Retreat

WHEN YOU LIVE IN A MILD CLIMATE, AN OUTDOOR FIREPLACE CAN EXTEND YOUR SWIMMING PLEASURES AS TEMPERATURES COOL.

LEFT FALLING WATER CAN BE AS RELAXING AS THE SOUND OF A CRACKLING FIRE.

OPPOSITE AN ARCHED TRELLIS AND CANDLE CHANDELIER ADD ROMANCE WITHOUT DETRACTING FROM THE FOCAL-POINT FIREPLACE. A SEATING AREA CLOSE TO THE FIREPLACE PROVIDES A RELAXING AND INTIMATE PLACE TO DINE.

LEFT THE BLOND STONE USED TO SURROUND THE POOL ALSO ADORNS THE PATIO NEXT TO THE HOUSE, PLAYING UP THE COUNTRY FRENCH THEME.

RIGHT RUSTIC BISTRO CHAIRS SUIT THE FRENCH THEME. UNDERFOOT, AROMATIC CREEPING THYME FILLS THE GAPS BETWEEN THE FLAGSTONES.

PAGES 212–213 A RAISED STONE PLATFORM SURROUNDS THE 45-FOOT-LONG POOL, PROVIDING SEATING ALL THE WAY AROUND. SPIGOTS SET INTO THE STONE WALL TURN THE POOL INTO A SPLASHING FOUNTAIN. CUSHIONED TEAK FURNISHINGS PROVIDE ANOTHER PLACE TO RELAX POOLSIDE.

This 45-foot-long swimming pool was already a popular respite, and for good reason. Its raised-ledge design, handsome natural stone surround, and splashing built-in fountains made it as beautiful as it is fun.

Adding a fireplace to the back of the poolside guesthouse allows the swimming pool to be used year-round. When temperatures dip during the evening hours, the fireplace can be lit, providing a cozy place to warm up after a swim.

A cushioned banquette with a table and chairs allows the fireplace area to also serve as a lovely spot for dining. An arched metal trellis will one day fill in with flowering vine, providing cooling shade during the day.

To make this area more in keeping with the French styling of the guesthouse, the fireplace features a carved stone surround and a stone hearth. A candlelit chandelier finishes this outdoor room with romantic flair.

chapter 6
a Cook's Create Fantasy

Alfresco Fashion

Add some of your favorite kitchen luxuries to a shady backyard pavilion.

LEFT THE SMOKER, HEATED BY A STONE FIREBOX BELOW, ALSO FEATURES STAINLESS-STEEL CUBBIES TO HOUSE WOOD SPECIES SUCH AS PECAN, HICKORY, AND MESQUITE; THE CHEF CAN BARBECUE USING THE FLAVOR OF CHOICE.

OPPOSITE THIS CLASSIC GARDEN PAVILION PROVIDES SHELTER FROM THE SUN AND RAIN AND ADDS A SENSE OF LUXURY TO THE BACKYARD.

The owners of this outdoor haven installed a stovetop, grill, smoker, warming drawer, fireplace, and a few cushy easy chairs inside an expansive brick pavilion, which makes just being in their backyard feel like a mini vacation.

The shelter's formal symmetry was designed to meld with the elegant garden setting and adds a touch of class to the landscape. A television, dining set, and fine-furniture-quality storage armoires create an atmosphere conducive to a relaxing afternoon or hosting catered events. The pavilion ensures shade from the sun as well as shelter from the rain.

Polished granite countertops ensure the cooking area remains beautiful and classic for years to come. Rough-cut edges blend the countertops with the brick and mortar interior walls, creating visual unity.

Wrought-iron chairs match the iron railing surrounding the pavilion while overstuffed outdoor seat cushions ensure the comfort of guests and family members. A carved-marble table complements the outdoor room's traditional styling and provides an excellent place to enjoy whatever mouthwatering dishes the chef has prepared.

THIS HEAVY CARVED MARBLE TABLE CAN WITHSTAND WIND AND RAIN AND LOOKS AS ELEGANT BARE AS IT DOES DRESSED IN FINE LINENS.

221

LEFT A 19TH-CENTURY TERRA-COTTA LUNETTE HANGING ABOVE THE SINK, AS WELL AS THE WEATHERED AND OIL-RUBBED BRONZE FAUCET, BRINGS CHARACTER TO THE VICINITY.

OPPOSITE THE SITTING AREA IN FRONT OF THE HEARTH IS PERFECT FOR AFTER-DINNER CONVERSATIONS AND CREATES A SENSE OF BEING INDOORS WITH ALL THE BENEFITS OF RELAXING OUTSIDE.

Desert Haven

It's no mirage. This desert paradise is primed with amenities to make cooling off, warming up, or partying a breeze.

LEFT The soothing sound of running water adds a sense of serenity to the surroundings.

OPPOSITE The kitchen bar brings the family together for a mouthwatering dish fresh off the grill. After an afternoon in the pool, adults can lounge in the sitting area next to the kitchen while kids play and swim in the pool to burn off the last of their energy.

LOW, BUILT-IN RETAINING WALLS PROVIDE A PLACE TO SIT AND ENJOY A HOT MEAL BEFORE CLAMORING BACK INTO THE POOL. THE BRICK STEPS AND FLOORING CREATE A PERFECT TRANSITION FROM POOL TO KITCHEN AND MAKE THE FOOD EASILY ACCESSIBLE.

An outdoor kitchen located adjacent to the pool and spa offers a perfect place to prepare a plate of hot food without missing out on any of the poolside fun. In this barely north-of-the-border backyard, a stainless-steel grill, sink, and cabinets make meal preparation easy and fun. The stucco walls add a Southwestern feel and mark the boundaries between pool, kitchen, and seating areas. The walls also house a perfect location for a fireplace to keep the nights warm and lit.

A cutout in the stucco wall creates an ideal place for a table between the pool and kitchen and enables anyone lounging in the spa or other play areas to come and get their food fresh off the grill.

Seating comes by way of Adirondack chairs strategically placed in front of the fireplace. Retaining walls plumped up with pillows ensure that everyone will have a place to sit. Behind the counter, the chef has a spot to prepare foods while still enjoying guests and family members.

Cooking Capers

ENJOY THE SUNSHINE AND THE SWIMMING POOL WHILE YOU GRILL A DELICIOUS MEAL FOR FAMILY AND FRIENDS.

LEFT THE ENTICING AROMA OF A HEALTHFUL AND TASTY MEAL GRILLED POOLSIDE MAKES ANY PARTY MORE FUN.

OPPOSITE A COMBINATION OF OVERHEAD AND SCONCE LIGHTING ENSURES THAT THE KITCHEN WILL BE USEFUL BOTH DAY AND NIGHT. THE PRACTICAL U SHAPE GIVES THE CHEF AMPLE COUNTER SPACE AND MAKES APPLIANCES EASILY ACCESSIBLE.

LOCATED NEXT TO THE SWIMMING POOL, THIS BEAUTIFUL OUTDOOR KITCHEN IS PERFECT FOR SERVING A SNACK OR BEVERAGE AND OFFERS A PLACE TO SIT AND CHAT WITH THE CHEF ON THE OPPOSITE SIDE OF THE BAR.

Located between the house and pool, an outdoor kitchen provides a place to enjoy the afternoon or grab a quick drink before heading back into the pool. These four kitchens show some of the possibilities.

The U-shape space shown here and on the preceding page makes moving around the kitchen convenient while keeping everything within easy reach. A gabled roof protects the kitchen from rain and offers shade to anyone grabbing a drink or making a snack. Marine-quality paint covers plywood cabinets and ensures durability. Stone countertops and stainless-steel appliances are highly functional and offer a sleek, modern look.

Located on opposite legs of the U, a sink ensures easy cleanup and a refrigerator keeps drinks and perishables cool. At center, the grill brings it all together and provides the perfect place to create a meal. With counter space on both sides, the chef has plenty of room to cook and serve guests.

(CONTINUED ON PAGE 232)

AMPLE COUNTERSPACE IN THIS OUTDOOR KITCHEN PROVIDES THE CHEF WITH PLENTY OF ROOM TO PREPARE THE MEAL AND TO SIT DOWN TO ENJOY IT WITH GUESTS OR FAMILY MEMBERS. BUILDING THE GRILL DIRECTLY INTO THE COUNTERTOP MAXIMIZES WORKSPACE.

While the summer kitchen was once located in a separate building to keep the house from becoming too hot when preparing meals, today's outdoor kitchens are designed to do much more.

This modern outdoor kitchen draws the family together outdoors for informal get-togethers and provides the perfect place for entertaining several guests or hosting a party. The well-stocked work area includes space for food preparation, cooking, cleanup, and storage, while providing the added thrill of being outdoors.

Weatherproof easy-care surfaces include ceramic tile countertops and a combination of concrete and brick flooring. For carefree cooking, stainless-steel controls combine with a wrought-iron grill to aid the chef in creating delicious meals. Contemporary, washable chairs located around the snack bar welcome diners to enjoy a mouthwatering steak or hot cheeseburgers fresh off the grill.

(CONTINUED ON PAGE 235)

OPPOSITE THE WHITE BEADED-BOARD CABINETS CREATE INTERESTING CONTRAST AGAINST THE STONE SURROUND THAT ENCOMPASSES MUCH OF THE KITCHEN. STAINLESS-STEEL APPLIANCES AND GRANITE COUNTERTOPS GUARANTEE THAT THE KITCHEN WILL REMAIN BEAUTIFUL THROUGHOUT THE SEASONS.

RIGHT CUSTOM CABINETRY ALLOWS FOR STORAGE OF COOKWARE AND SERVING PIECES, ALLEVIATING THE NEED TO LUG OUT ITEMS USED OUTDOORS.

A large gazebo gives this outdoor cooking area shelter from the elements as well as excellent views of the garden beyond. Stonework and beaded board line the cooking station and give design flair to the hardworking kitchen. The flagstone patio meshes perfectly with the rugged stone that houses the dishwasher and cabinetry. The white woodwork provides a simple and perfect contrast to set the doors and cabinetry apart from the rest of the kitchen.

The stainless-steel grill also offers a side burner for preparing side dishes such as pasta or steamed vegetables and gives the chef several options to create a delicious meal. A dishwasher and sink make cleanup quick and easy. Granite countertops add class and sophistication, and the durable surface will never wear out.

(CONTINUED ON PAGE 236)

DURABLE SURFACES
SUCH AS CERAMIC
TILE AND POLISHED
STONE ARE USED FOR
PROTECTION AGAINST THE
ELEMENTS AND MAKE FOR
EASY CLEANUP. THESE
SURFACES ALSO ADD A
SENSE OF LUXURIOUS
STYLE TO THE KITCHEN.

To create a chic outdoor kitchen to match your home, look to your home's exterior for inspiration. This kitchen's ornate detailing complements the home's Greek Revival styling and offers elegance as well as protection from the elements.

On the counters, a combination of ceramic tile and polished stone provide a sophisticated look and help create an environment conducive for entertaining dinner guests. A state-of-the-art stainless-steel grill combines with a pair of gas burners to provide plenty of cooking power. An undercounter refrigerator ensures plenty of uninterrupted counter space, leaving adequate room for food preparation and cleanup.

chapter 7
Entertain with Flair

Celebration Center

COOK, ENTERTAIN, CLEAN UP, AND RELAX—ALL IN YOUR OWN BACKYARD.

LEFT SECURED TO IRON STANDS STAKED INSIDE A PLANTER BOX, PILLAR CANDLES PROVIDE MOOD-ENHANCING ACCENT LIGHTING.

OPPOSITE THE GAZEBO BEHIND THE POOL IS A PERFECT PLACE TO COOK A QUICK MEAL WHILE KEEPING AN EYE ON GUESTS WHO ARE SWIMMING.

OPPOSITE AN OPEN-AIR DINING ROOM OPPOSITE THE COVERED DINING AREA IN THE GAZEBO ALLOWS VISITORS TO CHOOSE TO DINE WITH OR WITHOUT SHELTER.

RIGHT THE OUTDOOR KITCHEN OFFERS PLENTY OF SPACE FOR A CHEF TO COOK UP A MOUTHWATERING MEAL OR TO SIT AND ENJOY A GOOD BOOK.

d

Draw your friends and family outside by making your patio as inviting as your home's interior. In this Tulsa backyard, you'll find a fully equipped kitchen, two comfortable dining spots, a place to lounge, a place to swim, and a place to soak and soothe tired muscles.

The kitchen is tucked into a quaint little gazebo, protecting it from the elements. Equipped with a sink, garbage disposal, pullout trash bin, icemaker, storage space, and a grill, the kitchen has all the amenities of an indoor cooking center, with the bonus of being outdoors. Granite countertops and stainless-steel appliances are durable and easy to clean.

A cozy table and chair set nestled under the gazebo provides a shaded area to enjoy a quiet meal or escape from the sun or rain. A larger dining table a few yards from the pool offers open-air dining and is the perfect place to entertain dinner guests. Nearby lounge chairs and side tables shielded by large umbrellas offer a relaxing place to enjoy the evening.

An array of flower beds and large pots with flowers and plants brings color and life to the stone-paved space.

THE SPA, LOCATED CLOSE
TO THE HOUSE, IS AN
IDEAL SPOT TO UNWIND
AFTER A LONG DAY AND
CAN BE ENJOYED ALL
YEAR ROUND.

Backyard Clubhouse

CREATE A PARTY-PERFECT DECK THAT WILL ENTERTAIN FOR HOURS ON END.

LEFT BUILT-IN LIGHTING ON THE STAIRS LEADING TO THE DECK ENSURES THAT GUESTS CAN SEE WHERE THEY ARE GOING AFTER DUSK. THE LIGHTS ALSO CREATE A PERFECT AMBIENCE FOR A PARTY.

OPPOSITE STURDY WROUGHT-IRON RAILINGS, SOLID DECKING, AND THE BOLD, ROCKY TERRAIN ALL COME TOGETHER TO CREATE AN ENTICING LANDSCAPE.

BACKYARD CLUBHOUSE

A RAISED DECK WITH
A GARDEN BELOW
OFFERS NUMEROUS
AREAS FOR GUESTS TO
MINGLE AND ENJOY THE
PARTY, WHETHER IN THE
AFTERNOON, EVENING, OR
AT NIGHT. COMFORTABLE
SITTING AREAS, AN
INDOOR-OUTDOOR SPA,
A FIRE PIT, AND ENTICING
PATHWAYS ENSURE
THAT GUESTS WILL BE
THOROUGHLY ENGAGED.

Levels and levels of accommodating outdoor rooms make this backyard an entertainment utopia. In addition to the indoor-outdoor spa and the fire pit seating area, there are numerous walkways and paths that are just as inviting as the destinations to which they lead.

Meticulously placed, natural-looking boulders are the perfect building blocks for the spa and suit the large scale of the wooden deck. Stepping-stones that lead to the base of the deck create easy access to the spa as well.

The deck is mostly raised to meet the upper level of the home. Its stature and size make it ideal for entertaining. An octagon-shape extension of the raised deck houses a built-in stone fire pit and perimeter seating. The pillars supporting the deck convey a sense of permanence that meshes well with the rest of the landscape.

BACKYARD CLUBHOUSE

ABOVE THE UPPER LEVEL OF THE DECK OFFERS AN INVITING SPACE FOR CASUAL DINING WITH FAMILY OR GUESTS. RELAXING IN A CHAISE LOUNGE IS ANOTHER OPTION.

LEFT AN INSET DIAMOND PATTERN ADDS A STYLISH ELEMENT TO THE SURFACE OF THE DECK.

OPPOSITE PLENTY OF SEATING AROUND THE ELABORATE FIRE PIT GIVES GUESTS A WELCOMING AREA TO RELAX AND FEEL THE WARMTH OF THE FIRE WASHING OVER THEM.

Soothing Refuge

INFUSE YOUR URBAN BACKYARD WITH A SENSE OF PEACE AND TRANQUILLITY.

LEFT DRESSED IN ELEGANT CONTEMPORARY ASIAN STYLE, THE OUTDOOR DINING TABLE IS AS ATTRACTIVE AS ANY USED INDOORS.

OPPOSITE THE GURGLING FOUNTAIN AT THE BASE OF THE PAVILION ADDS SERENITY TO THE AREA AND PLAYS UP THE TRANQUIL THEME.

Influences from the Far East bring sophisticated Asian flavor to this California landscape. A stucco-covered concrete pavilion offers shade from the sun and a tranquil place to enjoy an evening meal. Furnished with a dining table that seats up to 12, the roofed room creates the perfect space for fine dining with a few favorite guests. Radiant heat, draperies, a TV, and a stereo offer diners all the luxury of being indoors while still being able to spend a wonderful afternoon or night in the warmth or the sun of under the glow of the moon.

A few steps down from the pavilion, a reflecting pool with bubbling water sends off a sound of serenity that echoes through the area. Lush ornamental grasses and some bamboo underscore the flavor of the Far East.

Welcoming Committee

Extend your outdoor entertaining season by adding outdoor rooms warmed by a roaring fire and a heated pool.

LEFT With its roofline, columns, and tongue-and-groove ceiling treatment, this pavilion echoes the Arts and Crafts style of the main house.

OPPOSITE The TV nestled into the cabinetry helps guests catch up on the latest news or sports scores while sitting at the bar.

Boasting a spot for lounging, bar-side seating, and a place for roasting marshmallows, this Cincinnati poolside pavilion offers all the comforts of home. A fireplace, sofa, and chairs furnish one end of the space, while a fully equipped kitchenette and small bathroom fill the other end.

The sloping shoulders of the fireplace are broad enough to block any harsh wind or sun but low enough to maintain the open-air feel. A TV nestled into a cutout in the bar area cabinets provides visitors seated at the bar a way to catch up on the day's events. Plenty of seating around the bar and cooking center offers a place for visitors to relax and enjoy the afternoon with a cold drink. Lounge chairs and tables sprinkled around the pool provide space to catch some sun or watch the kids splashing.

When a crackling fire and heated pool water aren't enough to warm the space, the water is turned off so pipes don't freeze. A set of folding doors draw closed to protect the appliances from the elements.

ABOVE THE SITTING AREA NEXT TO THE FIREPLACE IS A WARM, COMFORTABLE PLACE TO UNWIND AFTER A LONG DAY OR TO LINGER OVER CONVERSATION.

OPPOSITE THE PAVILION OFFERS A SHADED AREA WHERE SWIMMERS CAN RELAX OR GRAB A QUICK BITE TO EAT AFTER A FEW LAPS IN THE POOL.

Old-World Escape

VACATION IN YOUR OWN BACKYARD, SURROUNDED BY LUSCIOUS MEDITERRANEAN ACCENTS.

LEFT ITALIAN TILE ACCENTS THE STUCCO WALLS AND BRINGS MEDITERRANEAN FLAVOR TO THE OUTDOOR SETTING.

OPPOSITE THE FRONT GATE OFFERS A GLIMPSE OF THE WORLD YOU ARE ABOUT TO ENTER AS YOU PASS INTO THE COURTYARD BEYOND.

OLD-WORLD ESCAPE

THE STONE FIREPLACE IS CONDUCIVE TO ENJOYING A NICE EVENING MEAL AND ENSURES THE AREA WILL REMAIN WELL LIT AND WARM THROUGH ALL HOURS. THE CONCRETE TABLE RESEMBLES STONE AND CAN WITHSTAND STRONG WINDS AND RAIN.

Even if you live on one of the busiest streets in your city or if you have neighbors within close proximity, you can create a hidden escape from distractions and noise. Your portal to paradise may only be as far away as walling in your backyard to create a seemingly antiquated courtyard.

Spanish wooden windows, a stone bench, brilliant blooms, and a gurgling tiled fountain at the garden's entrance make it seem as if you are stepping straight from the home's interior into a Mediterranean village. Spanish music, soft candlelight, and bright flowers combine with stucco-covered walls to ensure a Mediterranean atmosphere in the outdoor gathering space. Bold blue and yellow Italian accent tiles stand out against the grayed yellow walls, further accentuating the Spanish flavor. Pillow-topped seating areas encourage guests to enter and enjoy. (CONTINUED ON PAGE 264)

LEFT An intimate seating area with wrought-iron furniture beckons on a quiet afternoon.

OPPOSITE Outdoor fabric separates the house and the dining courtyard. The quaint setting is perfect for enjoying a delicious meal. Spanish music and softly flickering candlelight create a European atmosphere.

Throughout the courtyard, aged urns filled with an array of colorful flowers beckon guests to see what the entire landscape holds. Native Carmel stone paths connect each outdoor room and bring a sense of unity to the landscape.

The outdoor dining room is just one place to stop and spend some time. Seating in front of the glowing fireplace provides a perfect spot to enjoy a meal with guests and linger over conversation. A nearby enclosed garden offers more intimate seating. Wall finishes, furnishings, and accessories boasting the same color palette ensure that each courtyard is visually connected to the next. Climbing vines throughout the landscape cover pergolas, arches, and walls, bringing an old-world atmosphere to the entire area.

OPPOSITE A 1930S DOOR, ITALIAN TILE, ARTWORK, AND A WEATHERED CHAIR ARE THE FIRST GLIMPSES OF EUROPE THAT A VISITOR CATCHES BEFORE BEING WHISKED TO THIS BACKYARD VILLAGE.

ABOVE A SMALL SITTING AREA IN ONE OF THE COURTYARDS OFFERS A PLACE TO TAKE IN THE LANDSCAPE.

Crowd Pleaser

Transform your landscape into an entertaining Mecca with inviting shade and sunfilled spaces.

LEFT The dining table seats up to eight and looks elegant and inviting when topped with a bouquet of garden flowers. Behind the table, lattice screens serve as privacy partitions.

OPPOSITE Sunlight and shadows seem to dance off the water, making the view from the house sparkling and enticing.

To make the most of the outdoor season, the owners of this Missouri home made their suburban backyard into a haven for entertaining. Multiple seating areas cluster around the sprawling pool, making it easy to share sultry summer days with friends and family.

Originally planned as a small exercise space, the pool was reconfigured into a 15×60-foot pool to accommodate lap swimming. The pool's sheer size makes it the focal point of the backyard, but it's also the stunning center of attention from inside the house, where large windows across the back of the home draw the pool's reflection in. Pool depth ranges from three to five feet, making it the perfect place to get a friendly game of water volleyball going.

A large gazebo at one end of the rectangular pool offers shade from the sun and room for a larger acrylic dining table. Lattice screens in place of walls provide a sense of enclosure while still enabling the warm breeze to glide through the room. Comfortable lounge chairs opposite the house offer a place for swimmers to dry off or relax in the sun.

A dining set near the back door offers a perfect place to enjoy morning coffee or an evening meal after a day in the pool. Changing areas added to the back of the garage offer guests privacy and a quick place to switch to swimming gear before jumping into the pool. A cedar fence meets safety regulations for fencing in swimming pools.

OPPOSITE BLOOMING PLANTS AND FLOWERS ADD A TOUCH OF LIFE TO THE AREA AND SPRUCE UP THE SURROUNDINGS.

ABOVE SHADED BY A FIBERGLASS ROOF, THE DINING SET INSIDE THE GAZEBO PROVIDES SHELTER FROM THE SUN AND A PERFECT PLACE FOR AN OUTDOOR DINNER PARTY.

CROWD PLEASER

COMFORTABLE CHAISE
LOUNGES OFFER A
RELAXING PLACE TO
SOAK UP SOME SUN OR
DRY OFF AFTER A SWIM.
TOWERING TREES OFFER A
BIT OF SHADE.

Tranquil Retreat

A SOOTHING COLOR'S PALETTE LENDS AN AIR OF SOPHISTICATION TO THIS GRACEFUL BACKYARD.

LEFT A DECORATIVE STONE URN FILLED WITH WHITE BLOOMING FLOWERS UNDERSCORES THE GARDEN'S GREEN-AND-WHITE THEME.

OPPOSITE WATER BUBBLING FROM A BRICK FOUNTAIN CREATES SERENE BACKGROUND SOUNDS AND MAKES THE AREA IDEAL FOR RELAXING WITH FRIENDS OR ENJOYING A FEW MOMENTS OF SOLITUDE.

OPPOSITE THE PLUSH CUSHIONS AND PILLOWS ATOP THE WICKER FURNITURE ADD JUST THE RIGHT AMOUNT OF WHITE TO THE AREA AND PROVIDE A COMFORTABLE PLACE FOR DINING. THE GRASS-AND-MOSS CENTERPIECES ADD SPLASHES OF NATURAL COLOR TO THE WHITE TABLECLOTH.

RIGHT WICKER FURNITURE OFFERS A SPOT TO KICK BACK AND ENJOY THE SURROUNDINGS.

When planning a space for outdoor entertaining, let the architectural style of your home and your home's interior décor inspire your decorating choices. The most enticing outdoor spaces feel like an extension of your home's interior.

In this backyard entertaining space, white and green make up the entire color palette. Leafy vines and white flowering plants spaced throughout the yard as well as white outdoor furnishings ensure a smooth visual transition from one outdoor room to another. Clever space planning divides the average size backyard into a combination terrace and outdoor dining room, a courtyard gathering space with a wall-size fountain, and a thriving herb garden.

On the terrace, formal seating areas with a birdbath water feature offer the perfect space for quiet contemplation. Seating under a pergola provides shading from the sun. Bubbling wall fountains add a touch of serenity and the sound gives each of the garden rooms a calming feeling. Wicker chairs and plush cushions make the courtyard ideal for informal conversation. Splashes of color, such as the red brick wall framed by greenery, give the green-and-white theme a bit of relief. The stone paths connecting the patio spaces are also made more inviting for guests with blooming vines and pale-tinted blooms.

Outdoor Opulence

RICH EUROPEAN ACCENTS MAKE THIS COURTYARD AN INVITING AREA FOR GUESTS AND FAMILY MEMBERS TO GATHER.

LEFT Terra-cotta pots, trellises, and raised-bed planters provide the perfect place to add a bit of color to the landscape and keep in perfect tune with one another.

OPPOSITE Blue and yellow hand-painted tiles adorn the fountain.

Outdoor living boasts indoor comfort and style in this patio room that extends living space halfway into the backyard. Moorish-style archways relay a European courtyard feel while framing views of a fountain, outdoor fireplace, and raised flower beds. The cobalt blue accent squares on the saltillo tile floor add a splash of brightness and visually connect the covered patio room to the courtyard beyond.

A comfortable seating area and a dining set allow guests to sit and chat over a nice meal or relax with a drink in the afternoon or evening. The covered area also ensures shade and comfort on a hot day.

A small sitting area, dining set, fire pit, and fountain create a welcoming atmosphere in the courtyard as well, beckoning guests to enjoy the light of the fire and the serene sounds offered from the gurgling water. Terra-cotta pots housing plants of different shapes, sizes, and colors mesh perfectly with the tile flooring.

OPPOSITE MOORISH-STYLE STUCCO ARCHES MARK THE TRANSITION FROM OUTDOOR ROOM TO OPEN COURTYARD. THE WALLS OFFER PROTECTION FROM SUN OR RAIN, WHILE THE AIRY COURTYARD IS PERFECT FOR ENJOYING A WARM SUMMER DAY IN THE SUN.

ABOVE SEVENTEENTH-CENTURY MONASTERY CHAIRS COMPLEMENT A TABLE MADE FROM AN ANTIQUE SPANISH CHURCH DOOR. AN INDIGO-DYED WOVEN RUG SOFTENS THE TILE FLOOR AND MAKES THE AREA MORE INVITING.

OUTDOOR OPULENCE

LARGE ARCHED WINDOWS
AND DOORWAYS MAINTAIN
THE SPANISH THEME AND
ALLOW COOL BREEZES
TO FLOW THROUGH
THE OUTDOOR PATIO.
LIGHTWEIGHT CURTAINS
CAN BE USED TO BLOCK
THE HOT SUN OR CALM A
GENEROUS BREEZE.

OPPOSITE THE OUTDOOR FIREPLACE BECKONS GUESTS WITH ITS LIGHT AND WARMTH ON COOL SUMMER EVENINGS AND CREATES AN ATMOSPHERE PERFECT FOR ENTERTAINING.

RIGHT BOUGAINVILLEA AND SWEET-SCENTED STAR JASMINE ENCOMPASS THE SIDE OF THE HOME, CREATING A LOVELY BOUNDARY FOR THE GATED COURTYARD.

INDEX

dare to dream
be inspired and make your dream a reality

GREAT
TRADITIONAL STYLE

GREAT **KIDS' ROOMS** COLLECTION

GREAT
COUNTRY FRENCH STYLE

GREAT
WINDOWS & WALLS COLLECTION

Better Homes and Gardens
Pool & Spa PLANNER

{ **Style** and **Inspiration** combine to bring you the best design ideas.
Look for these inspiring titles where home improvement books are sold. }